TRADITIONS • INGREDIENTS • TASTES • TECHNIQUES • 65 CLASSIC RECIPES

THE FOOD AND COOKING OF
COLOMBIA
& VENEZUELA

PATRICIA McCAUSLAND-GALLO

This edition is published by Aquamarine, an imprint of Anness Publishing Ltd, Blaby Road, Wigston, Leicestershire LE18 4SE.

Email: info@anness.com
www.aquamarinebooks.com; www.annesspublishing.com

If you like the images in this book and would like to investigate using them for publishing, promotions or advertising, please visit our website www.practicalpictures.com for more information.

UK distributor: Book Trade Services; tel. 0116 2759086; fax 0116 2759090; uksales@booktradeservices.com; exportsales@booktradeservices.com
North American distributor: National Book Network; tel. 301 459 3366; fax 301 429 5746; www.nbnbooks.com
Australian distributor: Pan Macmillan Australia; tel. 1300 135 113; fax 1300 135 103; customer.service@macmillan.com.au
New Zealand distributor: David Bateman Ltd; tel. (09) 415 7664; fax (09) 415 8892

Publisher: Joanna Lorenz
Editorial Director: Helen Sudell
Executive Editor: Joanne Rippin
Designer: Adelle Morris
Photography: Jon Whitaker
Food Stylist: Aya Nishimura
Props Stylist: Liz Hippisley
Editorial Reader: Lindsay Zamponi
Production Controller: Mai-Ling Collyer

Front cover image: Beef Turnovers (for recipe see page 32).

ETHICAL TRADING POLICY
Because of our ongoing ecological investment programme, you, as our customer, can have the pleasure and reassurance of knowing that a tree is being cultivated on your behalf to naturally replace the materials used to make the book you are holding. For further information about this scheme, go to www.annesspublishing.com/trees.

PUBLISHER'S NOTE
Although the advice and information in this book are believed to be accurate and true at the time of going to press, neither the authors nor the publisher can accept any legal responsibility or liability for any errors or omissions that may have been made nor for any inaccuracies nor for any loss, harm or injury that comes about from following instructions or advice in this book.

NOTES
Bracketed terms are intended for American readers.
For all recipes, quantities are given in both metric and imperial measures and, where appropriate, in standard cups and spoons. Follow one set of measures, but not a mixture, because they are not interchangeable. Standard spoon and cup measures are level. 1 tsp = 5ml, 1 tbsp = 15ml, 1 cup = 250ml/8fl oz.
Australian standard tablespoons are 20ml. Australian readers should use 3 tsp in place of 1 tbsp for measuring small quantities.
American pints are 16fl oz/2 cups. American readers should use 20fl oz/2.5 cups in place of 1 pint when measuring liquids.
Electric oven temperatures in this book are for conventional ovens. When using a fan oven, the temperature will probably need to be reduced by about 10–20°C/20–40°F. Check with your manufacturer's instruction book for guidance.
The nutritional analysis given for each recipe is calculated per portion (i.e. serving or item), unless otherwise stated. If the recipe gives a range, such as Serves 4–6, then the nutritional analysis will be for the smaller portion size, i.e. 6 servings. Measurements for sodium do not include salt added to taste.

Thanks to the following agencies for permission to use their images: Bridgeman Art: pp6b, 7t, 7bl, 7br. Corbis: pp8b, 9tr, 10bl, 12b, 15bm, 17t. Getty: p9b, 10t, 14tr, 15t, 18bl, 23, 41, 43, 59, 61, 109. Patricia Gallo McCausland: pp11all, 12t, 12m, 12tl, 13tr, 13tm, 13b,14bl, 14br, 14tr, 15bl, 15bm, 15br, 16tl, 16tr, 18br, 19bm, 19br, 21.

Contents

A culinary history

The neighbouring South American countries of Colombia and Venezuela are the wellspring of a flavourful, colourful mestizo (mixed-parentage) cuisine of the New World. The salty harvests of the ocean, the spices and fresh produce of the land, the clear air and the sunny climate help nurture a varied and vibrant cooking tradition that is celebrated by the creative, artistic souls of the people. This culinary heritage, passed from generation to generation, is deeply embedded in the lives of all Colombians and Venezuelans.

A shared tradition

The varied cuisine of Colombia and Venezuela is characterized by a wonderful blend of European cuisine, with aspects of African, Caribbean and indigenous traditions. The result is a wonderful mix of the best of each.

The old ways of life

The people who originally lived in this part of the world were successful farmers, fishermen, hunters and gatherers for centuries before the Spanish settlers arrived in the late 1400s. We know that native South Americans cooked foods such as conch, turtle and other seafood around 400BC, as remains of ceramic cooking pots dating from that era were found in San Agustín in Colombia. These people were hunters of large rodents such as guinea pigs, as well as deer, crocodiles, iguanas and

turtles; they also cultivated a huge variety of crops such as corn, yuca, yam, sweet potato, taro root, carob, squash, papaya, avocado, tomatoes, potatoes and beans. The tribes in the coastal areas grew these crops in well-organized fields or terraces climbing the steep hillsides of the lower Andes.

Both Colombian and Venezuelan natives prepared soups and stews with vegetables and roots mixed with fish, rather than meat, as there were few indigenous animals suitable for the pot. In the warm coastal areas they salted and smoked fish to preserve it. Corn was eaten both raw and cooked, as were sweet potatoes, and peanuts or a fiery hot pepper sauce was added to yuca roots to enhance their bland taste. The tribes surrounding the Orinoco River lived mainly on

Above: A reconstruction of a traditional Indian village at the edge of the Sierra Nevada de Santa Marta, once home to the indigenous Tayrona tribe.

Left: A woodcut illustration of an Indian food market at Cartagena, sometime in the 1500s.

Above: The arrival of Christopher Columbus on the Island of Guanahani in 1492.

Bottom right: A painting of a wedding dance at Guaduas, Colombia, 1834, shows guests wearing traditional costume.

Below: Simón Bolívar, who by 1819 had led Bolivia, Colombia, Ecuador, Panama, Peru and Venezuela to independence also freed the region's slaves.

its freshwater fish; they also ate iguanas and snakes, parrots, seagulls and ducks.

The native people cultivated plants for medicinal purposes as well as for food, and mainly led a healthy life, free of disease. They knew how to find ginger and turmeric, which was called the yellow tree, and used both these spices as medicines and in food. They were experts in working gold and making beautiful ceramic pots, which they traded for

The African influence
Europeans had already taken some of their food products into African countries, and the slaves they brought to Colombia and Venezuela from Africa had developed their own cuisine using the cheapest offcuts, such as pigs' trotters and ears, tripe, tongue and knuckles. They also brought the 'caldero', a large pot ideal for making soups and stew, in which anything and everything can be cooked. The slaves sold some of the foods they had prepared in the local markets, and so everyone learned to enjoy the colour and spice of Africa mixed with the traditions of the sunny Caribbean.

new foods with the Spanish. The Tainos tribe cultivated tobacco and other crops, and wove hammocks to sleep in. There is even evidence of large-scale salt mining from AD500 onwards at the Zipaquirá mines near Bogotá.

Venezuela was the first South American territory reached by Columbus in the late 15th century. When the first wave of conquistadors arrived in South America in the early 16th century, they found many different tribes with their own cultures. These people lived frugally, yet they experienced a life free of sickness and pain, but from then on the inhabitants' way of life, their food and customs were turned upside down. Although most of the original tribes died out, some elements of their cultures survive, in particular the foods they cooked, such as corn, yuca and potato.

European imports
Venezuela and Colombia were the main entry routes to South America from Europe, and so the people who lived there were also the first to experience the new foods brought by the conquistadors: olive oil, garlic, saffron and sausages such as chorizo, morcilla and butifarra. In return, the Spanish learned how to make casabe, the bread of the Indies (pan de las indias), from the yuca root, and took it with them on long voyages.

Many of the ingredients now seen as traditional in Colombia and Venezuela, such as plantains, rice, onions, oranges, mangoes, limes and coffee, were brought by settlers.

Geography and climate

The northern countries of South America greet the visitor with tropical sunshine and an array of blazing colour. The topography of the area, dominated by the Andes Mountains with their valleys and volcanoes, also contains tropical forests, flat plains and vast rivers. Colombia and Venezuela are blessed with an abundance of resources, and this has led to a very varied cuisine.

The High Andes

This huge mountain range crosses Colombia from south-west to north-east, and continues into western Venezuela, petering out near the Caribbean Sea. In Colombia, the Andean region, with its capital Bogotá, is the most densely populated part of the country, with plenty of popular tourist spots. The mountains contain warm valleys and snowy peaks, and produce a wide range of crops. Corn, sugar, coffee and vegetables of many varieties come from this part of the country, and recipes such as the renowned ajiaco (a creamy soup that used three types of potato) and many other highly calorific foods originate here. The cool climate means that the agricultural workers, toiling hard in the fields, need plenty of warming, sustaining food. Everything nutritious goes in the pot – even large ants (*hormigas culonas*), are eaten in the Santander part of this region, they taste like salted peanuts.

Santiago de Cali, the capital of El Valle del Cauca, is the centre of the main sugar-cane growing area, where two yearly crops are grown in the equable, warm climate, and this has become one of the most important agricultural regions in the country.

The warm Caribbean

The Caribbean zone, on the north coast of Colombia and Venezuela, has a humid tropical climate, but also contains a large desert area with natural salt mines, and mountains where coffee is grown. The great influx of international foods and seasonings that started when the conquistadors arrived on this coast in the 15th and 16th centuries, followed

Above: The countries of Colombia and Venezuela share not only a border and a coastline, but also the vast Amazon rainforest in the south, and very similar climates.

Left: Farms in an Andean valley near Llano del Hato, Venezuela.

Above: The Cocora Valley, in Quindío, in the central west of the country nestles between the Cordillera Central mountains of Colombia.

Above right: Traditional Spanish colonial facades in the World Heritage city of Cartagena, in the north west of Colombia.

by Asian, Middle Eastern and other European settlers, has made this area the centre of a flourishing cuisine. Most of the officers of the Spanish army settled in these pleasant coastal regions with their families and the slaves they brought to cook and to work the land.

In this region, ingredients such as plantain, yuca and corn are often used in both sweet and savoury recipes. Sweet black plantains in different forms, as well as yuca cakes (enyucado) and corn dumplings are served daily in many people's homes. Major cities in this part of Colombia include Cartagena de Indias, with its fortresses and walled city dating from the Spanish conquest; Barranquilla, which has a wonderful yearly carnival; Sincelejo, renowned for its sweets; and Montería, centre of the farming region.

Both Colombia and Venezuela also share a coastline on the shores of the tropical Caribbean Sea, which contains a huge variety of fish and is connected to Venezuela's

Maracaibo Lake through an artificial navigation canal. Venezuela's Caribbean district starts with the Lago de Maracaibo zone and ends in the far eastern states with the immense delta of the Orinoco River. It includes tropical beaches around the coastline, deserts, plains, valleys, mountains and forests, where farmers grow the local crops that are suited to the climate.

The Pacific coastline

The coastal region of Colombia, to the west of the Andes, borders the Pacific Ocean. It is a flat, humid territory of rainforest and farming land, now containing the largest number of African–Americans in the country, many of whom work on the banana plantations, as their ancestors did. Coconut milk flavours many of the dishes, such as ceviche (a mixture of marinated seafood) and fish soup.

Inland rainforests and flatlands

Further inland to the east, the tropical rainforest is fed by the great Amazon River. There are many good but unusual things to eat here, such as boa snake, turtles and their eggs, frogs' legs, conch and manioc. Brazilian influences can be felt from over the border, where yuca brava root is used to make bread.

The Llanos region, containing the ranching area of Colombia, is located in the eastern part of the country bordering Venezuela. The topography is perfect for cattle, with wide plains where the animals can roam and graze.

San Andreas and Providencia

These tiny islands (left) are located far out in the northern Caribbean, near Nicaragua, but actually belong to Colombia. They contain a large population of Afro-Caribbean people, who thrive on stews made with hot peppers, conch, crab and sweet coconut. They speak a language that is a mixture of English and French, called Patuá, or Creole.

Eating traditions

Colombian and Venezuelan cuisine is a real mixture of traditions from all around the world. The Spaniards and other Europeans who came to explore and never went back to Europe brought their own ideas on farming and cooking to this bountiful land full of colour, flavour and warmth. They intermarried with the local native population, so that many people have ancestors from Europe as well as other South American countries. They also brought African slaves, who had their own cooking techniques, which they shared with the indigenous population.

Family occasions

Colombians and Venezuelans are a very sociable group of people who see any event as the chance for a get-together, and food naturally becomes the focal point of these occasions. Usually at weekends, when the whole family is free, from grandparents to grandchildren, groups of family members meet up to eat, drink, chat and exchange news. Extended families do this at least once a week. No wonder most original recipes from Colombia and Venezuela make enough for 12 to 20 people. There are many dishes that can easily feed these numbers, often made in one or two large pots.

It is quite hard to give normal-sized portions for the recipes in this book, because although Colombians and Venezuelans usually have smallish families of four to six people, they rarely make dinner only for the exact number of people in the house. Children often bring friends over after school, or family members drop by for a chat and end up sharing supper, especially when traditional soups and stews are bubbling on the outdoor stove, filling the air with their strong fragrance.

Above: Freshly harvested coffee beans, picked when ripe, in a Colombian plantation.

Left: Large family gatherings, and generous portions, mean that Colombian market vendors can rely on their customers buying staple ingredients, such as these huge plantains, in bulk.

Below: The beautiful shiny skin of the cacao fruit.

Above: Corn fritters sold by street vendors.

Below top: Squash.

Below middle: Mango.

Bottom: Plantain chips.

Cooking for a crowd

The wonderfully varied produce of these countries gives local cooks the choice of a variety of ingredients that are usually mixed with guiso (a tomato and onion sauce, the staple seasoning), and rice, stock or coconut milk. This yields all sorts of different one-pot dishes that are ideal for feeding a whole crowd of people. The favourite recipes for big parties are sancocho (meat and vegetable stew, often served with rice) in the Caribbean coastal areas, ajiaco (chicken and potato soup) in the mountainous Andes, puchero (meaty stew) in the Paisa region or cazuela de mariscos (fish and shellfish stew) near the Pacific coastline. The best known rice dish, which is made everywhere in Colombia and Venezuela, is arroz con pollo, or chicken with rice, which includes whatever chopped vegetables are to hand, mixed with guiso and chicken pieces, all simmered in a bright yellow sauce flavoured with cumin. This dish can be made one day and reheated the next, for an even more intense flavour.

Even the warm climate does not stop anyone from eating hearty hot soups. It is traditional to make sure all the guests have a chance to see the dish of the day being prepared, which usually happens outdoors, on a large terrace, in the garden or on a farm, where the large pots are set over wood fires. The aroma of these concoctions fills the air and the mixture of generations brings laughter and noise. There is always music in the background, helping to transform any get-together into a party.

Thrifty food

The Spanish settlers brought with them a recipe for a thick soup or stew known as olla podrida – a real mixture of vegetables, meat, beans and stock that is set to simmer gently for hours until it has a melting consistency. The native people of Colombia and Venezuela made this recipe their own by using all the offcuts and cheaper parts of meat, and now

Fish and rice

As both countries have an extensive coastline, seafood is a staple ingredient. But it is not just eaten fresh from the sea – the tradition of salting and drying fish to preserve it and to intensify the flavour has existed for hundreds of years. Salt fish blends well with the bland, absorbent rice brought by the settlers in the 1500s.

There are hundreds of fish and rice dishes in Colombia and Venezuela: for instance, arroz de lisa, a basic rice dish with dried fish; arroz de camarón, made with dried prawns (shrimp); arroz de mariscos, a mixed seafood dish; and many more. African slaves brought great recipes for dumplings, which the inventive cooks of South America blended with dried seafood to make fish dumplings (buñuelos de bacalao). One of the most old and treasured fish dishes is known as viuda de pescado, a hearty mixture of dried fish, roots and tubers over plantain leaves on top of hot coals, where coconut milk is added to steam the dish to perfection.

the local version of olla podrida is made from poultry giblets, chickens' feet, pigs' trotters, pork and beef ribs, oxtail and many more lesser cuts. This mixture, known as sancocho, is made with whatever ingredients can be found in each region, always flavoured with guiso, and cooked for long periods of time in order to extract all the goodness from the very bony pieces of meat. Of course this gives the dish a flavour that white chicken meat or a lean cut of beef could never produce.

Over time, cooks began to add some small pieces of lean meat to sancocho, for extra goodness. However, the bony ribs and tails must still form a major part of the dish, as it is these frugal ingredients that give the soup its wonderful flavour and texture. Another variant arose around the mountainous zones of the

Above: Mangoes come in many varieties. These are plump and fleshy, yellow inside even when unripe and great with salt.

Andes, where all kinds of yellow, red and other varieties of potato grow well. These are added to the soup, creating a thicker mixture. Corn is another very popular ingredient for bulking up soups and stews.

In the coastal areas, coconut milk is usually included as part of the cooking liquid, and sancocho is more often based on the produce of the sea, such as octopus, conch, fish and shellfish. These soups are known as cazuelas.

Shopping for food

The street markets in Colombia are very organized places. They are used by the family cook, and also by restaurateurs and the owners of small supermarkets, who go along daily to buy all the ingredients they need in the restaurant or the store. Here everyone can inspect a vast range of produce, from meat and fish to vegetables and fruit, so that they can select the best by sight, smell and feel.

It is not only open-air markets that stock the best produce; supermarkets in both Colombia and Venezuela are a marvel too. They are often very large, and many of them are international European chains that have merged with native ones, and now carry all

sorts of ingredients from the local area as well as imported goods. Colombian and Venezuelan stores stock the most amazing fruit, vegetables, roots, tubers, nuts, herbs and spices, which grow prolifically in the clear air and pleasant climate of the mountains, as well as a vast variety of fish and shellfish, meat and game from the coasts and plains. Middle Eastern, Asian, African and European groups

Left: Green plantains, and far left, garlic and potatoes are all sold in huge quantities.

Below: Long canoes loaded with fruit and sugar cane, at a river market in Quibdo, Colombia.

Above: The fruit of the palm tree, chontaduro, is cooked in salted water for 1–2 hours and then eaten with salt or honey.

Above middle: Arepas are egg-filled empanadas, made of both yellow and white corn and sold in small sizes for outdoor parties and carnivals.

Above right: Fried beef empanadas are often made in the coastal areas and sold on street corners.

Below: A street stall's white and yellow corn arepas and empanadas, as well as sweet white corn and aniseed arepas, ready to be fried.

have mingled with the original native peoples, all bringing their own influence to bear on the stock carried by the supermarkets. The result is a fabulous range of foods to suit this all-embracing cuisine.

Street food

Markets in Colombia and Venezuela are not just for buying food, clothes and all the necessities of life. There is always a special part of the market where breakfast and lunch dishes are being prepared in open-air kitchens. Clients are usually local workers who are stopping off for a bite to eat before going to work, truck drivers who have transported the produce from farms to sell in the market, or even chefs from the restaurants, who pass by occasionally for a taste of traditional food such as masas (corn dough). In these kitchens, which are usually lined up next to each other, the cooks – mostly women – work

away during the night and early morning. They sell arepas (corn rolls filled with all kinds of savoury delicacies), empanadas (meat-filled pastries), bollos (similar to polenta), rice, eggs and Creole sauces.

One of the most popular dishes at these market stalls is recalentao, which usually includes white rice, fried sweet plantains and meat, with guiso or Creole sauce, and then some extras if desired, such as chicharrón (crispy fried pork strips), arepas and cheese.

The type of arepa on sale in the markets varies, depending on the area. On the northern Caribbean coast of Colombia the most common ones are egg-filled; in Venezuela they contain beef, tomato, cheese, or even chicken and avocados, a dish known as reina pepiada. In the Andean areas the best arepas are made of yellow corn, and these are known as arepa de choclo in Colombia, or chachapas in Venezuela.

Market masas

Many a market stallholder sells masas (ready-made dough) of corn or yuca, which is the main ingredient of everyday arepas, empanadas and carimañolas (meat fritters). The stallholders have their own large molinos, or grinders, where corn and yuca are ground after being soaked and cooked, and then the grain is formed into dough.

Festivals and celebrations

Colombia and Venezuela are countries where any event is enjoyed to its fullest, and each celebration involves great banquets that take many days to prepare. These are religious countries, and at least half the festivals commemorated throughout the year have a Catholic origin. But alongside the main Christian festivals, there are beauty pageants, carnivals and fairs all around the country to choose a local beauty queen and to celebrate a harvest of coffee or rice, sugar or corn.

New Year

As the year begins, everyone joins in New Year celebrations. In many places the custom is to place a human-sized figure made from rags outside the house and set it on fire at midnight to get rid of the past year's troubles. People celebrate with different drinks – light rum in the coastal areas, and aguardiente, an aniseed-flavoured strong spirit, in the inland areas. After this everyone sits down to eat traditional foods such as tamales, hayacas and pastels, which are varieties of pasty made of corn or rice or even both. Pork and chicken, potatoes and peas, guiso and seasonings are all placed in large plantain leaves, wrapped, and tied up to be cooked in a large pot.

Epiphany and Feria de Manizales

Less than a week goes by before the next holiday arrives. On 6 January, Three Kings Day (Epiphany), sweets (candies) are given to the children, while the adults celebrate by

Below: Chicken parcels are served at Barranquilla.

watching bullfights and partying afterwards. In the coffee-growing region of Viejo Caldas, one of its main cities, Manizales, holds a huge fair during the first week of the year, and chooses its Coffee Queen. During this week of bullfights and cultural activities, typical street foods are served, such as arepas, chorizo, chicharrones and a great bandeja paisa (a vast mixture of 13 traditional foods served on a tray), with plenty of aguardiente.

Carnaval de Barranquilla

February arrives and everyone gets ready for four days of carnival in Barranquilla and other cities. This carnival season is the pre-Lent way to let off steam, sometimes exceeding the normal boundaries of social correctness. The street food is of great importance during these four carnival days, as no one is supposed to work, even in the kitchen. Sancocho (soup) is the basic food,

Above: A life-size human effigy is set alight at New Year.

Above left: Colombian bullfighter, Luis Bolivar, performs at La Macarena bullring in Medellin.

Below: A street parade during the Feria de Manizales.

Above: A contestant in the Miss Colombia pageant.

Below and below right: The four-day carnival prior to Ash Wednesday began as a freedom day given to slaves in Cartagena by the Conquistadores. The costumes reflect what the person is trying to attach blame to or what they feel is taboo.

Below middle: Women work as a team to make hundreds of empanadas for a street festival in Bolivar.

maintaining everyone's energy ready for long nights of partying and dancing. The two basic types are trifasico sancocho, which includes beef, chicken and pork, and guandu (pigeon pea) sancocho, which is made of beans and salted meat. Snack foods for the daytime include butifarra con bollo (a kind of sausage sandwich), empanadas (little pastries), chuzo (meat skewers), arepa con huevo (egg rolls), carimañolas (meat pies) and more.

Semana Santa – Holy Week

Easter is known as Holy Week and is celebrated with processions in the streets. The main foods associated with Holy Week are sweets or 'dulces' that are sold at fairs. The majority of these sweets are prepared by African-Americans, who have passed their recipes from generation to generation by word of mouth. Whole families help to make delicious hard sugar candy with fruits from the region, such as papaya, coconuts, raspberries, figs and yellow currants.

Vallenato Festival

In April, the Vallenato music festival involves three days of partying, music and rum, plus the most delicious foods. Sancocho, chivo (goat meat), butifarra and many other dishes keep the party going. The intensely hot climate means that people need to drink lots of agua de panela (a lime-flavoured raw sugar drink), lemonade or the pungent, fermented corn and pineapple chicha.

Miss Colombia Pageant, November

During the month of November, the national beauty pageant brings people to the city of Cartagena de Indias. In this city, where the cooks maintain a wonderful repertoire of traditional dishes, there is a great focus on cooking and eating. On the streets, delicious snacks are on sale, such as arepas, seafood cocktails, empanadas and fried plantains.

Candle Day, 7 December

December brings Holy Mary Day or Candle Day, which is celebrated by lighting millions of candles outside houses at night. It is a beautiful sight to see the cities lit only with soft candlelight. The food for this day is also very special, including buñuelos (soft, cheesy fritters), natilla (a milky sweet dessert) and hojaldras (sweet deep-fried fritters).

Feria de Cali, 22–30 December

The year's end comes with festivals in Cali, where bullfights and cabalgatas (horse parades) are accompanied by music in the streets for all to enjoy. Tascas, restaurants set up on the street near the river, are the place for people to go out to eat. Meat from the wide plains is barbecued over wood or coals. Empanadas and patacones (fried plantain) are served with an array of ají (spicy) sauces. Champús, a cold drink made of lulo fruit, is sold on street corners, and aguardiente to make the party go with a swing. At dawn a bowl of sancocho is the favourite breakfast.

Classic ingredients

One of the hardest things for any visitor to these countries to comprehend is the sheer range of foodstuffs that grow in Colombia and Venezuela. Both places have such diverse climates within their borders that they can provide almost all the ingredients that are needed for this splendidly varied cuisine, including tropical fruits such as coconuts and bananas, staples such as yuca flour and corn, delicious local white cheese from the mountains, beef from the inland plains and coffee from the hill plantations.

Meat, poultry and game

The thrifty traditions of Colombia and Venezuela mean that most parts of animals are used, with nothing going to waste. People enjoy eating foods such as tongue, tail, offal, pork ears and trotters. Traditional delicacies such as pork fat are used to make chicharrones, a tasty street snack, and the bones give a fantastic flavour and a melting texture to soups and stews.

The more luxurious and expensive cuts of beef are enjoyed at their best in carne en posta, posta negra or asado negro, steak that is cooked until it is almost black outside and very tender and rare inside, served with a delicious, slightly sweet sauce. Two favourite beef dishes using lesser cuts are carne desmechada, made of skirt (flank) steak which is cooked, shredded by hand and flavoured with guiso; and carne en polvo, beef cubed and cooked in stock and then ground.

Pork often features as the main meat at a celebration meal. Lechona, a whole pig complete with the head, is roasted and served

as a party piece that will easily feed 50 people. The innards and blood are made into blood sausages and stews. If the pig has already been cut into pieces for cooking, the favourite pork dish is cañón de cerdo, a large fillet served with sweet sauce.

Free-range hens are the main ingredient in several sancochos, the staple dish of many Colombian families. Turkeys also feature in soups and stews, giving plenty of meat to feed a large family gathering. In the flatlands and the vast inland territories covered with

Above: A lobster fisherman selling his day's catch straight from his boat.

Top left: Street vendors sell their produce, including blood sausages that are already cooked and only need reheating.

Below from left: skirt (flank) steak, pork belly, chicken for a sanchoco, and squid.

Right: An array of vegetables on display at a fruit and vegetable wholesaler in the Colombian capital of Bogota.

Below from top to bottom: Prawns, clams, cuajada and costeno cheeses.

forest, many game animals and birds still roam and are sometimes hunted for food. These include crocodiles, rabbits, ducks and the capybara, a large, slow-moving animal that was traditionally eaten during Lent by special dispensation from the Catholic Church.

Fish and shellfish

With the long coastlines and massive rivers of both countries, it is no wonder that there is an immense variety of fish and shellfish in the local diet. Crab and lobster are particular favourites. Crab is most often found in rice dishes, coconut milk soups and au gratin, while lobster tails are barbecued or cooked in seawater and served with salad. There are plenty of other delicacies from the sea, such as conch, octopus, squid, oysters, clams, cockles, shrimp, prawns and many others that live in the warm waters around the coast.

The multitude of fish dishes includes those made with bocachico, a freshwater fish from the rivers, which is cooked in many different ways – in a stew, fried with slashed skin, dried or barbecued. Hundreds of other species of fish are caught and cooked, including red snapper, mackerel and catfish. One of the best ways to eat fish and shellfish is in the form of ceviche, which can be bought from many beachside stalls and restaurants.

Dairy products

Many different kinds of cheese are made in Colombia and Venezuela. The fresh, unsalted kind such as quesillo, which is a very crumbly white farmer's cheese, is often eaten for breakfast. Plain arepas are flavoured with a hard, salty cheese called queso costeño, which is sold in large blocks. A soft, chewy fresh cheese called cuajada is often served with sweets, raw sugar syrup and fruit.

Milky drinks and desserts include kumis, a sweetened sour-milk drink, and other drinks blended with fermented corn or oatmeal. Some, such as arequipe or dulce de leche, are made with milk that is heated with ground,

rehydrated rice and sugar, which thickens the mixture after hours of cooking. Colombian and Venezuelan families are also fond of milky desserts such as postre de natas (curdled milk pudding), tres leches (three-milk cake) and arroz con leche (rice pudding).

Vegetables and grains

Perhaps the most important ingredient of all in Colombian and Venezuelan cooking is corn, which is the basis of so many soups, stews, tarts and breads. Maiz pilao, made from a mixture of rehydrated and cooked corn kernels in different colours and sizes, is used for making arepas. The cooked kernels can also be transformed into chicha, a fermented pineapple, corn and sugar drink devised by the indigenous inhabitants of the Andes and still consumed today.

Yuca is a starchy tuberous root, also known as cassava or manioc, that is used to make a vast range of dishes, from breakfast foods and breads to sweets. Yuca bread can be mixed with cheese and formed into pandebonos (cheesy rolls), or shaped into a wreath for a special occasion and sprinkled with sugar. This versatile root can also be

made into a side dish when stewed with butter and cheese, or blended with cheese and eggs to make a soufflé, or even served as a dessert or sweet snack in the form of yuca balls, which are simply cooked, finely ground yuca root, fried and covered with syrup.

The Andes Mountains are the source of a rich variety of potatoes, which are cooked in many different ways: salted, boiled, fried, in soups and as part of many other dishes. With such a wide choice of local potatoes, the correct type and texture can always be found for each recipe, from floury and white to red, pink and yellow and waxy for salads.

Other vegetables commonly used in Colombia and Venezuela include squash and arracacha (which resembles a combination of carrot and sweet potato). Onions are a vital part of guiso or hogao seasoning sauces

and are found in many dishes; red or purple onions are used mainly around the coast, with ceviches and salads. Tomatoes, like onions, flavour almost every dish. Garlic and spices such as achiote, cumin, bay leaves, thyme, oregano and pepper, mixed with annatto, are part of many recipes and make up the powdered seasoning mixes sold in markets. Galinsoga, known in Colombian as 'guasca' is a herb similar to coriander that is often used.

Fruit

All kinds of fruits are eaten in Colombia and Venezuela, at all times and in all places – on the street, at the beach, bought from special fruit kiosks and stores, in restaurants and of course at home. Fresh fruit juice in a restaurant will arrive in a tall fancy glass, sweetened or unsweetened, but always freshly squeezed. One of the most popular fruits is mango, which is available all year round. But there are also pineapples, guavas, papayas, bananas, oranges, tangerines, limes, tamarind, soursop (also known as pawpaw or custard apple), chontaduro (hearts of the palm tree), mamoncillo (a cousin to the lychee), passionfruit and many more colourful, aromatic and delicious fruits.

Plantains are the kings of the region. These are typical tropical fruits used in savoury or sweet dishes because of their bland flavour. They resemble bananas, and can be used green and unripe, yellow and semi-ripe, or

Above, from left: Cassava, purple potatoes, onions, galinsoga.

Below, from top: Tamarind, papaya and soursop.

Left: Farmers set up roadside stalls near their land to sell produce direct to passers by.

Above, from top: Guava paste, plantains, suger cane, panela.

Right: Fruit stalls like this appear all over Colombia and Venezuela.

Far right: African sweets are sold in the Caribbean cities.

completely black and fully ripe. Dishes made with green plantains include fried circles (platanitos); fried, pressed and refried chunks (patacones); and grated plantain pressed into little patties (arañitas). Fully ripe black plantains are turned into sweet, fried, elongated strips about 1cm/½ in wide (tajadas) or plantain pie.

Coffee, chocolate and sugar

The richest coffee in the world is grown in the Colombian mountains, and is the country's biggest export. This plant grows at its best at altitudes above 1,200 metres/4,000 feet, where seemingly never-ending fields of green or red-coloured beans can be seen on the mountain slopes. Colombians and Venezuelans drink small cups of black coffee from the moment they open their eyes in the morning until late at night. At breakfast time, as in many other countries, coffee is mixed with hot milk and sweetened.

Colombian and Venezuelan cocoa is another top-quality product. Hot chocolate to drink is made with special chocolate bars that come in 1lb blocks, divided into 1oz squares. Each square makes one cup of the delicious morning or evening drink. Cooking and baking chocolate is also sold in blocks, and comes in

white, dark, milk, semi-sweet and unsweetened varieties. Coffee liqueurs are very popular after-dinner drinks, and make wonderful desserts.

Sugar cane, a widespread crop in Colombia, is important to both the economy and the cuisine. It is a vital part of a refreshing drink known as agua de panela, a mixture of water, ice, a block of raw sugar and limes. Sugar makes an instant dessert when added to all kinds of fruit, such as coconut (cocadas), papaya (caballitos de papaya, made of strips of candied papaya) or bocadillo veleño (guava and sugar paste wrapped in plantain leaves). Many kinds of sweets are sold at street stalls during Holy Week and at Christmas time many of them made to ancient recipes that are closely guarded family secrets.

To make agua de panela

Place a block of panela (hard raw sugar), about 450g/1lb in weight in a large pan with 475ml/16 fl oz/2 cups water and bring it to a simmer. Once the panela has dissolved fully, add 475ml/16 fl oz/2 cups ice and the juice of 2 limes. Mix well and serve on a hot day.

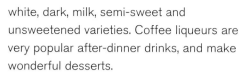

Street Food and Snacks

These wonderful little morsels are quick to make and easy to eat, whether at home or on the move, at any time of the day or night, for parties or for nights in!

The ideal solution for a hungry moment

Colombians and Venezuelans are always ready for a snack between meals, both mid-morning and at tea time. People tend to gather in family groups for a drink and something small and delicious to eat, or go out to pick up a snack from a bakery or from one of the many street carts or beach stalls. In the big cities, the streets are the meeting place for friends and relations alike, and almost every city has its speciality food sold on street stalls in traditional style.

Most of these snacks are based on a highly seasoned mixture of egg, cheese or meat such as sausage or pork ribs, often wrapped in cornbread or a tortilla, and topped with a spicy sauce. Four different sauces are included in this chapter, all based on strong-flavoured ingredients such as garlic, sweet chilli, tomatoes and onions with plenty of herbs. The vibrant flavours and colours reflect the atmosphere of Colombian and Venezuelan life.

These kinds of dishes are also very popular for a long, lazy breakfast, especially at weekends, when there is more time to sit around the table with a group of family members and enjoy a bigger breakfast than usual. Everyone is happy to sit for a while, eating, chatting and drinking hot chocolate or coffee, while savouring delicious homemade traditional foods such as arepas (cornbreads), pandebonos (cheese rolls) or empanadas (meat-filled turnovers). Most of these recipes would also be ideal for lunch, needing no more than a bowl of fresh fruit to follow.

Middle right: A Cartagenan woman, in a colourful traditional dress, sells fresh exotic fruits inside the old city.
Page 21: A waiter serves party food during carnival.

Egg-filled corn fritters
Arepas de huevo

These delicious double-fried corn fritters will send you off to work with energy for a whole day. Street vendors sell them in the old walled city of Cartagena de Indias, the magnificent jewel of the Caribbean, and visitors marvel at the egg cooked inside with the yolk soft or hard, as they wish.

1 Place the cornmeal and salt in a bowl and mix together. Add the warm water and stir in with a fork, then use your hands to blend the ingredients to a rough dough. Cover the bowl and set aside for 5 minutes.

2 Turn the dough out on to a work surface and knead for a minute to thoroughly mix.

3 Shape the dough into a roll and cut into six equal parts. Roll each piece into a ball. Place a ball of dough in an open plastic bag.

4 Flatten out the ball of dough to a disc about 10cm/4in across and 5mm/¼in thick. Remove from the bag. Repeat with the remaining balls.

5 Heat the oil in a deep pan. When it reaches 165°C/329°F, drop in the arepas one at a time and fry for 1–2 minutes. They will inflate on one or both sides. Remove them with a slotted spoon, taking care not to tear the sides. Drain on kitchen paper, with the inflated side up.

6 Break one of the eggs into a small cup. Using a sharp-pointed knife, make a 2.5cm/1in cut in the edge of one arepa and push the knife in to open the air pocket in the side.

7 Pour the egg into the pocket and immediately place the arepa back in the hot oil, with the opening at the top. Hold it in the oil for a few seconds until the egg begins to set, then let it fall into the oil and fry for 1–2 minutes, depending on how you want the yolk cooked.

8 Lift the aprepa out of the pan with a slotted spoon and drain on kitchen paper. Repeat with the remaining arepas and serve immediately.

Serves 6

175g/6oz/1½ cups pre-cooked white cornmeal

350ml/12fl oz/1½ cups warm water

750ml–1 litre/1¼–1¾ pints/ 3–4 cups oil, for deep-frying

6 small eggs

salt

Cook's tip If you want to make small, party-sized arepas, break all the eggs into a measuring jug and whisk them lightly together, then pour some of the egg into each pocket.

Energy 356kcal/1476kJ; Protein 9g; Carbohydrate 21g, of which sugars 0g; Fat 26g, of which saturates.4g; Cholesterol 179mg; Calcium29mg; Fibre 0.6g; Sodium 66mg

Creole egg tortilla
Tortilla de huevo a la criolla

Egg tortillas are sold on street corners and eaten for a breakfast on the go any day of the week. Creole sauce usually accompanies them at weekends and on special occasions, when breakfast will probably also include arepas, cheese and coffee.

1 First prepare the sauce. Heat the oil in a large pan, add all the ingredients and cook over medium heat for 7–10 minutes, or until the onions are translucent and the mixture has reduced to a thick sauce. Remove the bay leaves and keep warm.

2 Press the cooked rice into a coffee cup to mould each portion and turn out on to warm serving plates. Place in a warm oven.

3 Crack the eggs into a bowl and add the cream and salt. Mix well.

4 Melt the butter, or heat the oil, in a frying pan over medium heat, pour in the eggs in and cook for 3–4 minutes. When the tortilla is golden brown underneath, cover the pan with a large plate, flip the tortilla on to it and then slide back into the pan to cook the other side.

5 When cooked, slice the tortilla, add to the plates, and spoon the sauce on the side or over the tortilla and serve at once.

Variation To make scrambled egg rather than a tortilla, stir the eggs while cooking.

Serves 4–6

300–450g/11oz–1lb/2–3
  cups cooked white rice

8 fresh eggs

30ml/2 tbsp single (light)
  cream

15ml/1 tbsp butter or oil

salt

lettuce or parsely, to garnish

For the Creole sauce

30ml/2 tbsp oil

1 onion, sliced

2 tomatoes, peeled and sliced

2 garlic cloves, chopped

2 ají dulce chillies

2 bay leaves

10ml/2 tsp Worcestershire
  sauce

salt and ground black pepper

Energy 321kcal/1342kJ; Protein 13g; Carbohydrate 28g, of which sugars 4g; Fat 18g, of which saturates 5g; Cholesterol 317mg; Calcium 80mg; Fibre 1.2g; Sodium 156mg

Cheese fritters
Buñuelos

Makes 12

150g/5oz queso blanco (white farmer's cheese)

45ml/3 tbsp tapioca flour

30ml/2 tbsp precooked white cornmeal

7.5ml/1½ tsp sugar

2.5ml/½ tsp salt (less if the cheese is very salty)

1 small egg, beaten

1 litre/1¾ pints/4 cups oil, for frying

Traditionally eaten at Christmas, buñuelos are the kind of food you'd find in a home where grandma still does the cooking. They are also sold on the streets, in schools, breakfast kiosks, restaurants and bakeries, to eat with hot chocolate or cold drinks.

1 Place the cheese in a food processor and process for about 30 seconds, until finely shredded. Add the tapioca flour, cornmeal, sugar and salt to the cheese and mix.

2 With the motor running, drop the egg into the processor and continue mixing for 1 minute, until the mixture has formed a smooth dough and leaves the sides of the bowl clean.

3 Break off pieces of the dough and roll them into 2.5cm/1in balls with your hands. Do not press too firmly: they should be light and fluffy.

4 Heat the oil in a deep pan. When it reaches 165°C/329°F, drop in a few buñuelo balls: leave plenty of space, as they will expand to almost double their original size when cooked.

5 After cooking for about 30 seconds the balls will float. Lower the heat to 150°C/300°F and cook for a further 5–7 minutes or until golden. Drain on kitchen paper before serving.

Cook's tip You can make these a few hours in advance, but they are best eaten on the day they are made.

Energy 106kcal/440kJ; Protein 2g; Carbohydrate 7g, of which sugars 1g; Fat 8g, of which saturates 2g; Cholesterol 9mg; Calcium 46mg; Fibre 1g; Sodium 262mg

Cornbreads with cheese
Arepas de queso

These delicious cornbread fritters are sold from street stalls all over Venezuela and Colombia, grilled over hot coals and served on plantain leaves. The cheese may be either mixed into the dough or placed in the centre, so that it oozes out appetizingly as the moist arepa is wrapped in the leaf. In Venezuela arepas are stuffed with all kinds of fillings, such as beef, fish, beans or the very popular reina pepiada – a mixture of chicken and avocado.

Makes 8

175g/6oz/1½ cups precooked white cornmeal

350ml/12fl oz/1½ cups warm water

15ml/1 tbsp butter, softened

2.5ml/½ tsp Herb Sauce (*see* page 38), optional

225g/8oz queso blanco (white farmer's cheese) or mozzarella cheese, grated

salt

a little oil or butter for cooking

Cook's tips This amount of dough will make 24 mini arepas, about 2.5cm/1in in diameter. If you want to get ahead, you can freeze the arepas after shaping them. Cook them from frozen, allowing 3 minutes each side.

1 Place the cornmeal and salt in a mixing bowl and mix together with a fork. Add the warm water and butter (and Herb Sauce if using) and stir in with the fork, then use your hands to blend the ingredients to a rough dough. Cover the bowl and set aside for 5 minutes.

2 Turn the dough out on to the work surface, break it into pieces, add the grated cheese and knead for two minutes to make sure the cheese is evenly incorporated.

3 Shape the dough into a roll and cut it in half, then cut each half into into four equal pieces. Roll each of the eight pieces into a ball.

4 Place a ball of dough in an open plastic bag and using the palm of your hand, or a rolling pin, flatten it out to a disc about 10cm/4in across and 1cm/½in thick. Repeat with the remaining dough balls.

5 Lightly oil or butter a heavy frying pan or griddle set over medium heat.

6 Place the disc in the pan, and cook for about 2 minutes, then flip it over with a spatula and cook for a further 2 minutes, until golden.

7 Remove the cooked arepa from the pan, and repeat with the other seven discs of dough until all of them are cooked. If your frying pan is big enough you might be able to cook them two at a time. Serve while they are still piping hot and the cheese is melting.

Energy 223kcal/925kJ; Protein 7g; Carbohydrate 16g, of which sugars 0g; Fat 14g, of which saturates 6g; Cholesterol 20mg; Calcium 103mg; Fibre 0.5g; Sodium 122mg

Quick cheese rolls
Pandebonos

Delicious pandebonos are sold in the streets all over many Colombian towns. The stalls are usually set up near supermarket entrances, where the vendors can hook up their single-deck pizza ovens, in which the rolls bake best. Easy to make at home, their sweet, salty flavour is perfect with Colombian hot chocolate.

1 Preheat the oven to 220°C/425°F/Gas 7. Place all the ingredients in a food processor and process until the mixture feels smooth, with no lumps of cheese.

2 Leave the mixture to rest, covered, for 5 minutes. Turn the dough out on to the work surface and form it into a roll. Divide the roll into 12 pieces, then roll each piece with your hands into a sausage shape and join the ends to make an elongated circle.

3 Place the rolls on a thick or double baking sheet and bake in the preheated oven for 10–15 minutes, or until crisp underneath and their tops are lightly golden. Serve immediately, still warm, with coffee or hot chocolate.

Cook's tip You can keep the dough in a sealed bag in the refrigerator, and just roll as many pieces as you need. It will keep perfectly for three days. If the chilled dough starts to break up when you knead it, add a little milk.

Makes 12

350g/12oz queso blanco (white farmer's cheese), grated or feta cheese, crumbled

75g/3oz/⅔ cup tapioca flour

90g/3½oz/scant 1 cup pre-cooked yellow cornmeal

15ml/1 tbsp sugar

5ml/1 tsp salt (less if cheese is very salty)

1 egg

Energy 142kcal/594kJ; Protein 7g; Carbohydrate 14g, of which sugars 1g; Fat 7g, of which saturates 4g; Cholesterol 36mg; Calcium 110mg; Fibre 0.2g; Sodium 286mg

Green plantain chips
Platanitos

Serves 2–4

1 large green plantain
oil for deep frying
salt

Cook's tip Don't try to fry too many pieces of plantain at a time or they will stick together and cook unevenly.

Platanitos are best when they're eaten hot, straight out of the frying pan. Street vendors slice the plantains on home-made mandolines on their stalls and fry them in large pans of oil, and hundreds of little brown paper bags are filled with these crisp, paper-thin chips for passers-by to eat as they walk around town.

1 Cut the ends off the plantain and peel it. Cut long, thin slivers of the plantain along its length, using a mandoline or a vegetable peeler.

2 Heat 5–7.5cm/2–3in oil in a large pan. When the oil reaches 180°C/350°F drop a few of the plantain strips in, lengthways, one by one (as if they were diving), so that they don't stick to each other.

3 Fry the plantain strips, stirring continuously, for 1 minute or until lightly golden.

4 Remove the strips from the pan with a slotted spoon and drain on kitchen paper.

5 Repeat with a few more plantain strips until all of them are cooked. Sprinkle with plenty of salt and serve immediately.

Energy 238kcal/989kJ; Protein 1g; Carbohydrate 15g, of which sugars 3g; Fat 20g, of which saturates 2g; Cholesterol 0mg; Calcium 5mg; Fibre 0.7g; Sodium 2mg

Beef turnovers
Empanaditas de carne

Empanaditas are a staple street food and are also served at parties and in school cafeterias. You can prepare the filling ahead of time if you wish and store it in the refrigerator. Made with wheat flour dough and fried, empanaditas can be any shape, although half moon are the most popular.

1 To make the dough, place all the ingredients in a food processor and process for about 1 minute, until the dough leaves the sides of the bowl clean. Wrap in plastic and chill.

2 To prepare the filling, heat the oil in a large heavy pan over medium-high heat. Add the onion, carrot and red pepper, cover and cook for 5 minutes.

3 Meanwhile, put the meat in a bowl and add the chilli, coriander, Worcestershire sauce, garlic, cumin, salt and pepper. Mix well, then add the seasoned meat to the onion mixture and cook for 5 minutes, stirring.

4 Add the stock and potatoes to the pan and cook for 15–20 minutes more, or until the potatoes are soft and the stock has been absorbed. Set aside to cool completely before filling the empanaditas.

5 Roll out the dough to a rectangle 5mm/¼in thick, using a pasta machine or a rolling pin. Use cookie cutters to cut out 24 desired shapes; round is the traditional shape.

6 Place a teaspoonful of filling on one half of each pastry round, brush the beaten egg over the other half and fold it over. Seal tightly.

7 Heat the oil to 180°C/350°F in a deep pan and fry the empanaditas in small batches until light golden (about 40 seconds). Do not let them touch while cooking and turn to cook evenly. Remove with a slotted spoon and drain on kitchen paper. Serve immediately.

Cook's tip The filled and shaped empanaditas can be frozen, uncooked, for up to 3 months if well sealed. When you are ready to use them cook from frozen as above.

Makes 24

For the dough

450g/1lb/4 cups plain (all-purpose) flour, plus extra for dusting

20ml/4 tsp sugar

15ml/1 tbsp baking powder

10ml/2 tsp salt

115g/4oz/½ cup butter or 75g/3 oz/½ cup lard

60ml/4 tbsp ice cold water (120ml/4fl oz/½ cup if using lard)

For the filling

15ml/1 tbsp oil

50g/2oz/¼ cup chopped onion

50g/2oz/¼ cup grated carrot

50g/2oz/¼ cup grated red (bell) pepper

350g/12oz lean beef, finely chopped

½ chilli, chopped

15g/½oz/¼ cup chopped coriander (cilantro)

15ml/1 tbsp Worcestershire sauce

5ml/1 tsp chopped garlic

pinch of cumin seeds, toasted

120ml/4fl oz/½ cup beef stock

2 potatoes, diced

1 egg white or yolk, or whole egg, lightly beaten

salt and ground black pepper

oil for frying

Energy 273kcal/1134kJ; Protein 6g; Carbohydrate 18g, of which sugars 1g; Fat 20g, of which saturates 4g; Cholesterol 28mg; Calcium 40mg; Fibre 0.8g; Sodium 135mg

Pork and beef corn turnovers
Empanaditas vallunas

The dough, or masa, used for empanadas is traditionally prepared by soaking dry corn overnight, then cooking, cooling and grinding it. Sometimes it is soaked again for a day after cooking. This recipe uses precooked yellow cornmeal, which makes life much easier.

Makes 24

For the sauce

10ml/2 tsp oil

3 spring onions (scallions), finely chopped

2 small tomatoes, peeled, seeded and diced

3 garlic cloves, chopped

1.5ml/¼ tsp ground cumin

1.5ml/¼ tsp salt

pinch of achiote paste or turmeric

For the filling

150g/5oz pork shoulder, cut in 5mm/¼in dice

150g/5oz beef skirt (flank) steak, cut in 5mm/¼in dice

pinch of ground cumin

pinch of achiote or turmeric

250ml/8fl oz/1 cup beef stock

1 small waxy potato, cut into 5mm/¼in dice

2 small yellow potatoes, cut into 5mm/¼in dice

salt and ground black pepper

For the dough

475ml/16fl oz/2 cups water

10ml/2 tsp oil

10ml/2 tsp salt

300g/11oz/2 cup pre-cooked yellow cornmeal

1.5 litre/2½ pints/6 cups oil for deep-frying

lime wedges and Valluno Sauce (see page 39), to serve

1 Place all the sauce ingredients in a medium sauté pan and cook, covered, over medium-low heat for 20–25 minutes. Set aside.

2 For the filling, mix the pork, beef, cumin and achiote, or turmeric, in a pan and season with salt and pepper. Add the stock, bring to the boil and cook, covered, over low heat for 1 hour.

3 Reserve 15ml/1 tbsp of the sauce, then add the rest to the meat, with the potatoes. Cover the pan and cook for a further 30 minutes. Some potatoes will disintegrate; that is the way it is supposed to be. Leave the filling to cool while you prepare the dough.

4 Place the water, oil, reserved sauce and salt in a large pan, cover and bring to the boil. Uncover, lower the heat to minimum, then start to whisk in the cornmeal. When it begins to stiffen, change the whisk for a wooden spoon.

5 When the cornmeal is incorporated, remove the pan from the heat, turn the mixture out on to a work surface and leave it to rest for 5 minutes, covered with clear film (plastic wrap).

6 Knead the dough with your hands for about 3–5 minutes. Roll a piece of dough (about 30ml/2 tbsp) and place between two sheets of plastic. With a rolling pin or the base of a pan, flatten it to a thickness of about 1.5mm/⅙in. (You should almost be able to see through it.)

7 Remove the top sheet of plastic and place about 7.5ml/1½ tsp of filling in the centre of the flattened dough. Using the lower sheet of plastic as support, fold over the dough to form a half-moon shape. Firmly press the edges together. Trim to a neat semi-circle and peel off the plastic. Add the trimmings to another piece of dough to make the next empanada.

8 Heat the oil to 180°C/350°F in a deep pan and fry the empanadas in small batches for 2–3 minutes, turning once. Remove with a slotted spoon and drain on kitchen paper. Keep them warm while you cook the rest, and serve with lime wedges and Valluno Sauce.

Cook's tip If the dough tears while you are flattening it, return it to the remaining dough, knead for another 2 minutes, then try again.

Energy 169kcal/698kJ; Protein 3g; Carbohydrate 2g, of which sugars 0g; Fat 16g, of which saturates 2g; Cholesterol 8mg; Calcium 3mg; Fibre 0.3g; Sodium 187mg

Spicy beef sausages
Butifarras

Serves 4–6

450g/1lb beef skirt (flank)

115g/¼lb pork belly

1 garlic clove, chopped

7.5ml/1½ tsp black pepper

1.5ml/¼ tsp ground cumin

pinch of ground allspice

12.5ml/2½ tsp salt

100ml/3 ½fl oz/½ cup water
   (if piping)

natural sausage casing

Cook's tip You can also use Press 'n' Seal wrap. Follow the manufacturer's instructions.

Butifarras are enjoyed at carnival time, when they are eaten on the streets, served with cornbread rolls called bolos. With the right equipment, either a piping bag, or a sausage-making machine, and casings, you can also make them at home.

1 Dice the meats, place into a food processor with the garlic and spices and 7.5ml/1½ tsp salt and add the water if piping. Process until smooth. If using a sausage-making machine, pipe the mixture, knotting it every 2.5cm/1in.

2 If using a piping bag, rinse the casings and place in a bowl of warm water. Select a piping tube and fit a casing over the tip, pushing down as much as you can so it forms an accordion-like pleat on the tip. Keep wetting the casing as you work. Tie a piece of string close to the opening of the tip, then apply pressure to the bag with one hand and stuff the casing, pulling it from the tip as you go. It helps if two people do this. Don't over-stuff; if it bursts, tie it off at that point and start again.

3 When the casing is full, tie it off, then tie again every 2.5cm/1in to form the sausages. Repeat with the remaining mixture.

4 Fill a large pan with water, add the remaining 5ml/1 tsp salt and bring to the boil. Add the sausages and simmer, covered, for 15 minutes.

5 Drain the sausages and serve hot or cold, with Tomato and Onion Sauce (see page 39).

Energy 181kcal/755kJ; Protein 21g; Carbohydrate 0g, Fat 11g, of which saturates 4g; Cholesterol 57mg; Calcium 9mg; Fibre 0g; Sodium 880mg

Crunchy pork fritters
Chicharrones

Chicharrones are one of Latin America's best-loved, if most fattening, foods. They can be made in tiny squares to scatter over a dish of rice and beans, or in larger, longer pieces, as here, to eat on their own as a snack.

1 With a very sharp knife, cut the skin of each strip of pork, so that it will stay flat while cooking. Rub with bicarbonate of soda and set aside for 10 minutes.

2 Place the pork in a heavy pan, cover with water, bring to the boil and cook over medium heat until all the water evaporates.

3 Once the pan is dry the pork will begin to render its fat.

4 Sprinkle the meat with salt and continue to cook over medium heat for 5–7 minutes, turning the pork occasionally, until all the fat has run out and the chicharrones are browned and crisp. Remove from the pan and serve.

Serves 4–6

675g/1½lb fatty pork belly strips, 5mm/¼in thick (6–8 strips)

2.5ml/½ tsp bicarbonate of soda (baking soda)

2.5ml/½ tsp salt

Energy 290kcal/1206kJ; Protein 21g; Carbohydrate 0g, Fat 23g, of which saturates 8g; Cholesterol 80mg; Calcium 7mg; Fibre 0g; Sodium 652mg

Hot chilli sauce
Ají Antioqueño

This hot and spicy sauce, or ají, is a staple of Colombian cuisine. It's eaten with everything, from chorizo to empanadas, patacones and all kinds of meats. Keep it in a jar in the refrigerator for up to two weeks, to use on the spur of the moment.

Makes 300ml/½ pint/¼ cups

2–3 ají dulce chillies, seeded, or 1 small red (bell) pepper, chopped

1 habañero chilli, seeded

120ml/4fl oz/½ cup vinegar

1–2 spring onions (scallions), finely chopped

1 small onion, finely chopped

45ml/3 tbsp chopped coriander (cilantro)

5ml/1 tsp sugar

30ml/2 tbsp oil

salt and ground black pepper

1 Put the chillies in a blender with the vinegar and 120ml/4fl oz/½ cup water and blend until smooth. Transfer to a jar and add the remaining ingredients, seasoning to taste.

2 Chill the sauce for a couple of hours before using, to allow the flavours to blend. Store in the refrigerator for up to a week.

Herb sauce
Chimichurri

This fresh-tasting sauce is served with grilled meat all over Latin America. You can also use it as a marinade for meat. According to one story it gets its name from an Irishman, Jimmy McCurry, who joined the fight for Argentina's independence in the 19th century.

Makes 250ml/8 fl oz/1 cup

65g/2½oz/2½ cups parsley leaves

40g/1½oz/1½ cup coriander (cilantro) leaves

2 spring onions (scallions), chopped

15ml/1 tbsp vinegar

10ml/2 tsp lime juice

2 garlic cloves, finely chopped

120ml/4fl oz/½ cup oil

2.5ml/½ tsp salt

1.5ml/¼ tsp ground black pepper

1 Place all the ingredients in a food processor and process until you have a well-blended mixture.

2 Allow to sit for 10–15 minutes for the flavours to develop, and serve, or store in the refrigerator for up to a week.

Hot Chilli Sauce: Energy 400kcal/1651kJ; Protein 4g; Carbohydrate 22g, of which sugars 20g; Fat 31g, of which saturates 4g; Cholesterol 0mg; Calcium 78mg; Fibre 3.9g; Sodium 22mg.
Herb Sauce: Energy 1123kcal/4618kJ; Protein 4g; Carbohydrate 4g, of which sugars 3g; Fat 121g, of which saturates 14g; Cholesterol 0mg; Calcium175mg; Fibre 3.6g; Sodium 34mg.

Valluno sauce
Ají Valluno

Serve this mild chilli sauce with all sorts of empanadas – you will end up eating more sauce than empanada, it is so delicious. Like aji antioqueno, and hogao o guiso, this sauce is made in large quantities and kept in the refrigerator for using as and when it is needed.

Makes 150ml/½ pint/1¼ cups

75ml/2½fl oz/⅓ cup white vinegar

75ml/2½fl oz/⅓ cup water

10ml/2 tsp lime juice

1 small habañero chilli, seeded and very finely chopped

1–2 spring onions (scallions), finely chopped

1 small onion, very finely chopped

1 small tomato, peeled, seeded and very finely chopped

90ml/6 tbsp chopped coriander (cilantro)

5ml/1 tsp salt

7.5ml/½ tbsp oil

1 Mix all the ingredients together in large bowl.

2 Set the sauce aside for at least 1 hour before serving, for the flavours to blend.

Tomato and onion sauce
Hogao o guiso

This is probably the most important recipe in all Colombian and Venezuelan cuisine and is used in many recipes, with minor regional variations. The sauce can be prepared ahead of time and kept in the refrigerator for up to five days.

Makes 150ml/6 fl oz/1½ cups

30ml/2 tbsp oil

4 tomatoes, peeled, seeded and chopped

2 small onions, finely chopped

1–2 spring onions (scallions), finely chopped

30ml/2 tbsp finely chopped ají dulce chillies

30ml/2 tbsp finely chopped coriander (cilantro)

2 garlic cloves, chopped

15ml/1 tbsp Worcestershire sauce

pinch of sugar

2.5ml/½ tsp salt

1.5ml/¼ tsp ground black pepper

Place the oil in a large heavy pan over medium heat. Add all the remaining ingredients and cook for 10–12 minutes, covered, stirring occasionally, to make a chunky sauce.

Valluno Sauce: Energy 133kcal/551kJ; Protein 3g; Carbohydrate 9g, of which sugars 8g; Fat 8g, of which saturates 1g; Cholesterol 0mg; Calcium 64mg; Fibre 1.8g;Sodium 1989mg.
Tomato and Onion Sauce: Energy 393kcal/1632kJ; Protein 5g; Carbohydrate 25g, of which sugars 21g; Fat 31g, of which saturates 4g; Cholesterol 0mg; Calcium 92mg; Fibre 5.3g; Sodium 1199mg

Soups

Colombian and Venezuelan cuisine contains a variety of wonderful soups that are ideal as a starter for a long lunch, or as the main course.

A daily bowl of goodness

Most Colombians and Venezuelans, from the chilly mountain slopes to the tropical shores, enjoy a bowl of soup as a first course at lunchtime. Despite the heat of the coastal areas, it is always served warm. Soup is also the favourite dish for serving at most large family gatherings, as it is perfect for cooking in a large pot in the open air.

There are many varieties of soup in this inventive cuisine. Some are eaten for breakfast, such as changua (eggs poached in milk), while others, such as sancochos (so hearty they are almost a stew) and cazuelas (thinner soups), are perfect for lunch or for dinner. The lighter kinds are prepared with stock, while those eaten as the most filling part of a meal are prepared with coconut milk or even based on eggs. Bones usually flavour the stock, depending on the soup; often the tail is used for a fantastic rich savoury taste, or rib bones and pigs' trotters. Free-range (farm fresh) hens are used for chicken-flavoured soups, and a good Colombian or Venezuelan cook will start with a fresh bird, so these soups can be quite time-consuming to make. In these busy days, good quality ready-made chicken stock or whole cooked chickens from the store can be used too. Adding the right herbs is very important, as these often define the dish.

Some vegetables crop up in almost every soup: potatoes, yuca, butternut squash, and plantains, for instance. When green plantains are used they are usually peeled before adding to the stock, but when ripe ones are called for they are cooked separately with the skin on, in order to keep the soup from becoming too sweet.

Right middle: A traditional town in the High Andes.
Page 41: A street theatre artist performs during a parade in Bogota, Colombia.

Morning soup
Chanqua

Serves 4

1 litre/1¾ pints/4 cups water

475ml/16fl oz/2 cups milk

1 spring onion (scallion), thinly sliced

30ml/2 tbsp finely chopped coriander (cilantro)

1 garlic clove, peeled

4 eggs

4 slices of toast

salt and ground black pepper

This simple, warming soup is very popular in the Andes, where it is very cold in the mornings all year round, and it makes a sustaining breakfast. My paternal grandmother was from the mountainous region of Tolima and my father loved this soup as a midmorning snack, especially at weekends.

1 Put the water and milk into a pan and add 15ml/1 tbsp each of the sliced spring onion and chopped coriander and the garlic clove. Season with salt and pepper.

2 Bring the milk mixture to the boil, reduce the heat to a minimum and simmer for 10 minutes.

3 Remove the pan from the heat and pass the milk through a sieve. Return the strained liquid to the pan and turn up the heat to medium.

4 Warm four soup bowls and place 5ml/1 tsp coriander and 15ml/1 tbsp spring onion in the bottom of each one.

5 When the soup is bubbling, crack the eggs one by one into a cup and gently slide them into the hot liquid. Poach for 1 minute, then lift out the eggs and lay one in each bowl.

6 Ladle the hot soup over the eggs and serve immediately, accompanied by slices of toast.

Energy 221kcal/993kJ; Protein 15g; Carbohydrate 21g, of which sugars 7g; Fat 9g, of which saturates 3g; Cholesterol 239mg; Calcium 229mg; Fibre 1.3g; Sodium 301mg

Lentil and smoked fish soup
Sopa de pescado seco y lentajas al coco

This soup is typical of the Pacific coast, where hundreds of varieties of fish are caught, and many are smoked or salted to make transporting them to the open-air markets easier. Among the most popular species are a type of catfish called barbinche – or drumfish. You need to soak the lentils overnight.

1 Place the lentils in 1.2 litres/2 pints/5 cups water and leave to soak overnight. The next day, cover the fish in water and soak for 20 minutes. Drain it, remove any bones and shred the flesh. Set aside.

2 Drain the lentils and put half the soaking water into a medium pan with the coconut milk, lentils, green pepper, achiote or turmeric and culantro or coriander leaves.

3 Bring the soup to the boil and simmer, covered, for 30 minutes, until the lentils are cooked through but still whole.

4 Add the fish, Tomato and Onion Sauce, plantain pieces and diced potatoes to the pan and simmer over medium to low heat, half covered, for a further 30 minutes, or until the plantain is cooked through. Serve the soup straight away, with white rice.

Serves 4

450g/1lb/2 cups brown lentils

225g/8oz smoked catfish, snook, mullet or other ocean fish, skin removed

400ml/14fl oz/1⅔ cups coconut milk

¼ green (bell) pepper

2.5ml/½ tsp achiote or turmeric

2 culantro leaves or a handful of coriander (cilantro), plus extra for garnishing

1 quantity Tomato and Onion Sauce (see page 39)

1 green plantain, cut into 1cm/½in pieces

450g/1lb potatoes, peeled and cut into 1cm/½in dice

300–450g/11oz–1lb/2¾–4 cups cooked white rice, to serve

Energy 803kcal/3408kJ; Protein 45g; Carbohydrate 136g, of which sugars 16g; Fat 13g, of which saturates 2g; Cholesterol 26mg; Calcium 172mg; Fibre 14.2g; Sodium 1094mg

Seafood chowder
Cazuela de mariscos

This is one of my favourite warming soups. If you buy your seafood ready prepared, it can be made in minutes. The coconut milk can be fresh, frozen or canned, but if canned, make sure it's milk not cream. Serve with patacones (plantain fritters).

1 Heat the oil in a large, heavy pan and add the onions, red pepper, garlic, achiote or turmeric, Old Bay Seasoning (see Cook's tip) and bay leaves. Season with salt and pepper and cook, covered, for 4 minutes.

2 Mix the coconut milk with the stock and whisk in the flour until smooth. Add the mixture to the pan and bring to the boil, stirring.

3 Add the octopus to the pan and simmer, covered, over low heat for 20–25 minutes. Then add the sherry, clams, prawns and squid. Cook for a further 5 minutes.

4 Sprinkle in the parsley and coriander, and bubble for 30 seconds, then serve.

Cook's tip Old Bay Seasoning, originally from Maryland, USA, is now sold around the world, but if you can't find it you can make your own. Blend together 15ml/1 tbsp bay leaf powder, 37.5ml/2½ tbsp celery salt, 7.5ml/1½ tsp mustard powder, 7.5ml/1½ tsp black pepper, 2.5ml/½ tsp ground nutmeg, 2.5ml/½ tsp ground cloves, 2.5ml/½ tsp ground ginger, 2.5ml/½ tsp paprika, 2.5ml/½ tsp ground chilli, 1.5ml/¼ tsp mace and 1.5ml/¼ tsp cardamom. Store in an airtight container.

Serves 4–6

15ml/1 tbsp olive oil

1 small onion, coarsely grated

2 spring onions (scallions), sliced

1 red (bell) pepper, grated

2–3 garlic cloves, crushed

2.5ml/½ tsp achiote or turmeric

5ml/1 tsp Old Bay Seasoning

2 bay leaves

475ml/16fl oz/2 cups coconut milk

475ml/16fl oz/2 cups fish stock

30ml/2 tbsp flour

350g/12oz cooked octopus

50ml/2fl oz/¼ cup dry sherry

350g/12oz shelled clams

450g/1lb king prawns (jumbo shrimp), peeled

350g/12oz squid, thinly sliced

15ml/1 tbsp parsley, chopped

25ml/1½ tbsp coriander (cilantro), finely chopped

salt and ground black pepper

Energy 229kcal/1263kJ; Protein 46g; Carbohydrate 14g, of which sugars 7g; Fat 6g, of which saturates 1g; Cholesterol 353mg; Calcium 177mg; Fibre 0.9g; Sodium 1007mg

Fish and tomato soup
Sancocho de cabeza de pescado

Serves 4–6

2 small fish heads

900g/2lb white fish fillets, such as hake or haddock

juice of 2 limes

2 garlic cloves, crushed

4–5 tomatoes, peeled and seeded

15ml/1 tbsp olive oil

1 onion, thinly sliced

1 small red (bell) pepper, coarsely grated

60ml/4 tbsp tomato purée (paste)

2.5ml/½ tsp Old Bay Seasoning (see page 46)

1.5ml/¼ tsp achiote or turmeric

50ml/2fl oz/¼ cup red wine

450g/1lb cockles or clams

5ml/1 tsp sugar

30ml/2 tbsp parsley, chopped

30ml/2 tbsp coriander (cilantro), chopped

salt and ground black pepper

3 limes, quartered, to serve

This soup is a favourite in Colombia and Venezuela. These days fish heads are less easy to get hold of, but they really help the soup's flavour. We catch our own fish, and are often asked for fish heads by others who want to make this 'fish head' soup.

1 Rub the fish heads and fillets with lime juice and crushed garlic. Set aside for 10 minutes. Chop the tomatoes, retaining their juice.

2 Heat the oil in a large pan over medium-high heat. Add the onion and red pepper and cook, covered, for 5 minutes. Add the tomato purée, Old Bay Seasoning, achiote or turmeric, and salt and pepper to taste. Sauté for 2 minutes.

3 Pour in the wine and deglaze the pan, then add the fish heads, cockles or clams, tomatoes

with their juice, sugar and 2.4 litres/4 pints/10 cups water. Bring to the boil then lower the heat and simmer for 30 minutes.

4 Cut the fillets into strips or chunks 2.5cm/1in wide and add to the soup. Cover and cook for 5–7 minutes more, until the fish is just cooked.

5 Stir in half the chopped parsley and coriander and cook for a further 2 minutes. Serve immediately, sprinkled with the remaining herbs and accompanied by wedges of lime.

Energy 282kcal/1183kJ; Protein 44g; Carbohydrate 10g, of which sugars 8g; Fat 7g, of which saturates 1g; Cholesterol 89mg; Calcium 101mg; Fibre 1.8g; Sodium 1105mg

Hearty chicken soup
Sancocho Valluno

This substantial soup is often made in very large quantities as it's popular at family gatherings on farms in the countryside, where free range hens will have been running around – in fact, they are sometimes cooked with unlaid eggs still inside them. On occasions like this, the dish is usually cooked outside over a wood fire. Flavoured with achiote and pungent culantro leaves, its distinctive smoky smell infuses the house with a distinctive and irresistible Colombian aroma.

1 Cut the chicken in half with a large, sharp knife, and place in a large pan or stockpot. Add the coriander sprigs, culantro leaves, if using, spring onions, onion, carrot, achiote or turmeric, garlic and pepper.

2 Pour 3 litres/5 pints/12 cups water into the pan, and bring to the boil, then cover, lower the heat and simmer until the chicken is tender – about 1½ hours, or 2–3 hours for an older bird.

3 Lift out the chicken, cut it into bite-sized pieces and set aside, covered with 250ml/8fl oz/1 cup of the stock to keep it moist.

4 Top up the pan with extra water to make up to 1.75 litres/3 pints/8 cups. Season the stock with salt, add the plantain and cassava and simmer, half covered, for 20 minutes.

5 Add the Tomato and Onion Sauce to the pan together with the potatoes, cover the pan and cook for a further 20 minutes over low heat, until all the vegetables are tender.

6 Transfer the chicken pieces with the stock to a clean pan and heat very gently to warm through. Arrange portions of chicken on four side plates, with a small banana, an avocado quarter and a portion of rice on each.

7 Ladle the soup into warmed bowls, sprinkle chopped coriander over each, and serve alongside the plates of chicken, banana, avocado and rice.

Serves 4

1.3–1.8kg/3–4lb free-range (farm fresh) chicken

10 coriander (cilantro) sprigs plus 45ml/3 tbsp chopped coriander, plus extra to garnish

4 culantro leaves, chopped, if available (see Cook's tip)

2 whole spring onions (scallions)

1 onion, quartered

1 carrot, halved

5ml/1 tsp achiote or turmeric

1 garlic clove, chopped

2.5ml/½ tsp ground black pepper

15ml/1 tbsp salt

1 green plantain, peeled and cut into 1cm/½in slices

450g/1lb cassava, peeled, quartered and cut into 5cm/2in chunks

1 quantity Tomato and Onion Sauce (*see* page 39)

6 medium potatoes, peeled and halved lengthwise

4 small bananas, whole

1 avocado, quartered

300g/11oz/2¾ cups cooked white rice, to serve

Cook's tip If you can't find culantro, increase the amount of fresh coriander (cilantro).

Energy 899kcal/3799kJ; Protein 45g; Carbohydrate 144g, of which sugars 34g; Fat 20g, of which saturates 4g; Cholesterol 131mg; Calcium 108mg; Fibre 9.6g; Sodium 935mg

Chicken, corn and potato soup
Ajíaco Bogotano

This soup originated with the conquistadors, who cooked together any ingredients they could find, adding lots of chilli to add flavour. Galinsoga, which Colombians call guasca, or 'gallant soldier', can be replaced with bay leaves.

Serves 6

2 litres/3½ pints/8 cups chicken stock

2 skinless chicken breast fillets

1 spring onion (scallion)

bunch of coriander (cilantro)

2 whole corn on the cob, cut into chunks

12 small white floury potatoes, peeled and sliced

12 medium waxy potatoes, peeled and chopped

6 small red potatoes, peeled and cut into 2.5cm/1in chunks

90ml/6 tbsp fresh, chopped or 45ml/3 tbsp dried galinsoga, or 4 fresh or 2 dried bay leaves, crushed

salt and ground black pepper

90ml/6 tbsp capers, rinsed and drained, and 120ml/4fl oz/½ cup double (heavy) cream, to serve

1 Pour the chicken stock into a large pan and add the chicken, spring onion and coriander. Season with salt. Bring to the boil over medium heat and simmer, covered, for 20 minutes.

2 Remove and reserve the chicken breasts from the stock, and discard the spring onion and coriander. Add the corn and sliced white potatoes to the pan and simmer for 45 minutes, then remove the corn chunks from the pan and set them aside.

3 Chop or shred the chicken breasts and set them aside with the corn.

4 Add the rest of the potatoes and galinsoga or bay leaves, and simmer, uncovered, for a further 30 minutes, until the floury potatoes have broken down and made the soup creamy. Season to taste and add the chicken and corn.

5 Serve immediately, with the capers and cream in bowls at the table to stir into the soup.

Energy 332kcal/1398kJ; Protein 17g; Carbohydrate 40g, of which sugars 5g; Fat 13g, of which saturates 7g; Cholesterol 62mg; Calcium 42mg; Fibre 3.3g; Sodium 67mg

Oxtail soup
Sancocho de cola

This soup is usually served with the meat on the bones, although it is almost falling off them, because it is so tender after the long, slow cooking. Oxtail is a cheap cut of beef which is full of flavour and makes a soup that everyone really enjoys.

1 In a large pan over medium-high heat, brown the oxtail for 5 minutes. Add the red pepper, coriander sprigs and 2 culantro leaves, if using, with 3 litres/5 pints/13¼ cups water.

2 Bring the water to the boil then skim, lower the heat and simmer, half covered, for about 2 hours, or until the meat is very tender.

3 Add the corn, green plantain and cassava to the pan together with the remaining culantro leaves, finely chopped. Season with salt and pepper and simmer, covered, for 15 minutes.

4 Add the pumpkin to the pan with the Tomato and Onion Sauce and cook for a further 15 minutes, until all the vegetables are tender.

5 Add the finely chopped coriander to the pan and cook for 2 minutes more, then serve in warmed bowls, accompanied by cooked rice.

Cook's tip Culantro is the leaves of the herb *Eryngium foetidum*, which is native to Colombia, but cultivated worldwide. If you can't find it, simply increase the amount of coriander (cilantro) in this recipe.

Serves 4–6

1.8kg/4lb oxtail, cut into pieces

¼ red (bell) pepper

10 coriander (cilantro) sprigs, plus 45ml/3 tbsp finely chopped fresh coriander

4 leaves culantro, if available, chopped

2 corn on the cob, each cut into 4 pieces

1 green plantain, peeled and cut into 1cm/½in pieces

500g/1¼lb cassava, peeled and cut into 5cm/2in pieces

450g/1lb pumpkin, peeled and cut into 2.5cm/1in pieces

1 quantity Tomato and Onion Sauce (*see* page 39)

salt and ground black pepper

300g/11oz/2¾ cups cooked white rice, to serve

Energy 616kcal/2600kJ; Protein 40g; Carbohydrate 69g, of which sugars 9g; Fat 22g, of which saturates 1g; Cholesterol 0mg; Calcium 82mg; Fibre 1.2g; Sodium 423mg

Pigeon pea soup
Sancocho de guandul or guandú

This delicious soup is a chunky chowder made with pigeon peas, also known as gungo peas, which have a nutty, earthy flavour and are very popular in Latin America. If you can't find pigeon peas, use black-eyed beans instead. You can feed an army with this delicious, slightly sweet and savoury soup.

Serves 4–6

300g/11oz/1½ cups dried pigeon peas or black-eyed beans

225g/8oz beef jerky

225g/8oz beef ribs, cut into 2.5cm/1in pieces

225g/8oz pork ribs, cut into 2.5cm/1in pieces

225g/8oz pork shoulder, cut into 1cm/½in dice

1 corn on the cob, cut into 4 pieces

15ml/1 tbsp salt

350g/12oz potatoes, peeled and cut into 1cm/½in dice

350g/12oz peeled cassava, cut into 1cm/½in dice

350g/12oz peeled yam, half cut into 1cm/½in and half into 2.5cm/1in dice

1 ripe plantain, peeled and cut in to 5mm/¼in dice

1 quantity Tomato and Onion Sauce (*see* page 39)

1 Soak the dried pigeon peas or black-eyed peas, overnight in a large bowl of water.

2 Soak the beef jerky in water overnight too, or boil it in a small pan for 20 minutes. Discard the water and cut the beef into 1cm/½in dice.

3 Drain the pigeon peas and place in a large pan with 2.4 litres/4 pints/10 cups fresh water, place over high heat, bring to the boil, then reduce the heat and simmer for 1 hour, or until tender.

4 Preheat the oven to 220°C/425°F/Gas 7. Spread all the meats out together on a large baking tray and put them in the hot oven for 20 minutes, or until lightly browned.

5 Add the browned meat to the pan of peas, together with the pieces of corn. Season with salt, cover the pan and simmer gently for another 40 minutes.

6 Add the potatoes, cassava, yam, and plantain to the pan, and simmer for a further 40 minutes until the vegetables are tender.

7 If the soup is not thick enough when the vegetables are done, take out some of the large pieces of yam, mash them with a fork and return them to the pan.

8 Add the Tomato and Onion Sauce to the pan, stir through, and simmer for a further 2 minutes before serving in warmed bowls.

Energy 773kcal/3264kJ; Protein 53g; Carbohydrate 92g, of which sugars 9g; Fat 24g, of which saturates 8g; Cholesterol 109mg; Calcium 95mg; Fibre 8.2g; Sodium 1321mg

Tripe soup
Mondongo

Mondongo is one of Colombia's favourite foods and is often cooked in most households and in men's clubs. Men get together to sample and compare their recipes, and even set up associations in honour of this renowned dish. This recipe is an adaptation of the one my mother was given over 40 years ago when I was a child. Nowadays you can buy tripe perfectly cleaned and ready to use.

1 Wash the tripe well in plenty of water, then drain and rub with bicarbonate of soda. Place in a dish, cover with fresh water and set aside, covered, for 20 minutes.

2 Remove the tripe from the water and, with a stiff-bristled brush, brush the tripe to remove any unwanted loose debris. Rub the tripe with the lime halves, leave it to sit for 10 minutes, then wash it again.

3 Place the tripe, oxtail, pork and chorizo in a large pan. Add the bay leaves, cumin and 1.5 litres/2½ pints/6¼ cups of water to the pan. Season with pepper, bring to the boil, then lower the heat. Skim, then simmer, covered, for 2 hours, adding extra water if necessary.

4 Remove the pan from the heat, strain off the stock and reserve it. Cut the pieces of tripe in half, and pick the meat off the oxtail bones. Return all the meats to the pan.

5 Add the Tomato and Onion Sauce, potatoes, yam and cabbage to the pan. Pour in the strained stock, adding water if necessary, to cover all the ingredients. Season to taste with salt and bring to the boil.

6 Simmer the soup for 30 minutes, or until the vegetables are tender. Stir in the parsley and coriander, correct the seasoning and serve.

Cook's tip The initial cooking of the meat can be done in a pressure cooker, if preferred. It will need about 30 minutes.

Serves 4–6

450g/1lb tripe, cut in 2.5cm/1in pieces

2.5ml/½ tsp bicarbonate of soda (baking soda)

2 limes, halved

450g/1lb oxtail, cut into pieces

225g/8oz pork shoulder, cut into 5mm/¼in dice

1 chorizo, 15cm/6in long, cut into 5mm/¼in dice

2 bay leaves

7.5ml/1½ tsp ground cumin

1 quantity Tomato and Onion Sauce (*see* page 39)

2 medium potatoes, peeled and cut into 5mm/¼in dice

275g/10oz yam, peeled and cut into 5mm/¼in dice

115g/4oz/1 cup shredded cabbage

60ml/4 tbsp chopped parsley

30ml/2 tbsp chopped coriander (cilantro)

salt and ground black pepper

Energy 354kcal/1486kJ; Protein 31g; Carbohydrate 25g, of which sugars 5g; Fat 15g, of which saturates 5g; Cholesterol 128mg; Calcium 92mg; Fibre 2.6g; Sodium 445mg

Caribbean soup
Sancocho costeño trifásico

Serves 8–10

4 spring onions (scallions), chopped

2 medium onions, chopped

115g/4oz kale, chopped

150g/5oz carrot, chopped

4 green chillies, chopped

1 celery stick, chopped

3 garlic cloves, crushed

5ml/1 tsp black pepper

5ml/1 tsp achiote or turmeric

5ml/1 tsp allspice

5ml/1 tsp ground cumin

45ml/3 tbsp oil

675g/1½lb beef ribs, cut into short pieces

675g/1½lb pork ribs, cut into short pieces

1 free-range (farm fresh) chicken, jointed

450g/1lb chicken wings

500g/1¼lb cassava, peeled and cut into 5cm/2in chunks

1 green plantain, peeled and cut into 6 pieces

675g/1½lb red (russet) potatoes, peeled and quartered

500g/1¼lb yam, peeled and cut into 5cm/2in chunks

450g/1lb pumpkin, peeled and cut into 5cm/2in chunks

225g/8 oz sweet potato

2 corn on the cob, each cut into 4 pieces

45ml/3 tbsp coriander (cilantro), finely chopped

1 unpeeled ripe plantain, cut into 6 pieces

salt

450g/1lb/4 cups cooked white rice, and 3 limes, quartered, to serve

This is a lovely soup for a special family occasion. The broth is served in bowls, while the meats and vegetables are presented on large platters. Everyone puts meat and vegetables in their soup, and then adds rice and a squeeze of lime juice.

1 Put the spring onions, onions, kale, carrot, chillies, celery, garlic, black pepper, achiote or turmeric, allspice and cumin into a food processor and process to a coarse-textured paste. Rub the paste into the meats and set aside for 10–20 minutes.

2 Heat the oil in a very large pan over medium-high heat and add the pieces of meat in small batches, browning on all sides. Transfer to a clean bowl as they are done.

3 When all the meat is browned, return it to the pan with any remaining seasoning paste and add 7 litres/12 pints/30 cups water. Bring to the boil, then lower the heat, cover and simmer for 2 hours, or until the meats are tender. Remove the chicken pieces from the pan as they are done and set aside.

4 When the meat is cooked, remove the ribs from the pan and set aside. Season the stock with salt to taste, then add the cassava and green plantain and cook, covered, for 20 minutes. Add the potatoes, yam, pumpkin, sweet potato, corn and coriander.

5 Cook the soup for a further 25 minutes, or until all the vegetables are very tender.

6 Meanwhile, bring 1 litre/1¾ pints/4 cups water to the boil in a separate pan. Drop in the unpeeled slices of ripe plantain, cover and simmer for 25 minutes. Drain and keep warm.

7 Strain the soup and discard any bones. Place all the pieces of meat on one serving platter and the vegetables on another.

8 Serve the broth in bowls, accompanied by plates of white rice and lime wedges, together with the plates of meat and vegetables.

Energy 916kcal/3863kJ; Protein 57g; Carbohydrate 106g, of which sugars 8g; Fat 32g, of which saturates 11g; Cholesterol 175mg; Calcium 116mg; Fibre 5.3g; Sodium 212mg

Main Dishes

These main course recipes are based on the fabulous fresh fish and farmed meat that are enjoyed by Colombian and Venezuelan families.

Rib-sticking food with finger-licking sauces

The inland, hilly or even mountainous regions of these two countries are the source of most of the more substantial dishes described in this chapter. The people living in these cooler inland areas need plenty of good food to see them through the working day – for example, the Andean region is where the most bandeja paisa (a huge platter of meat, beans and rice) is eaten – whereas the people in the hotter coastal areas traditionally eat more fish and salad.

The Atlantic and Pacific Oceans bordering Colombia and Venezuela, as well as the mighty inland rivers, are full of delicious fish and shellfish. This is often prepared with coconut, or simply cooked over a wood fire, wrapped in plantain leaves, and then cut into bitesize pieces dressed with lime and oil, ceviche-style. The fishermen who work the coastal waters simmer their fish in salty sea water, and serve them on platters with rice, plantains and salad.

Huge meat-based breakfasts and midday meals are common in the Andes, whereas evening meals are usually small, just consisting of coffee and arepas (cornbread fritters) or hot chocolate and buñuelos (cheese fritters). The recipes in the following chapter are suitable for a few people or can be adapted for a crowd, and will satisfy the biggest appetites.

Right middle: The secluded fishing village and white sandy beaches of Grand Roque Island in the Los Roques National Park Archipelago, Venezuela.
Page 59: A street stall sells fresh fruit in Cartagena.

Lobster salad
Ensalada de langosta

On the islands of the Caribbean, freshly caught lobsters are cooked in seawater and nothing else. At home, we season the cooking water to add flavour, and make a tangy dressing for this delicious salad, served with buttery, perfectly ripe avocados.

1 Pour 2–3 litres/3½–5¼ pints/8–13¼ cups water, depending on the size of the lobsters, into a large pan. Add the coriander, chopped spring onions, peppercorns and salt to the pan.

2 Bring the water to a fast boil, add the lobsters, cover and simmer for 10 minutes. Remove the lobsters from the pot.

3 Whisk together all the ingredients for the dressing and set aside.

4 When they are cool enough to handle, cut the lobsters in half lengthways and remove the meat. Slice thinly and mix with the dressing. Halve the avocados and remove the stones. Divide the lobster salad among the avocado halves and serve immediately.

Cook's tip If you are using live lobsters, chill in the freezer for 10 minutes before cooking. This sends them to sleep, so that when they enter the boiling water, movement is minimal.

Serves 4

4 small live lobsters or 225g/½lb lobster tails

5 coriander (cilantro) sprigs

4 spring onions (scallions), chopped

5ml/1 tsp crushed peppercorns

15ml/1 tbsp salt

2 medium avocados

For the dressing

30ml/2 tbsp vinegar

30ml/2 tbsp lime juice

30ml/2 tbsp water

2 red ají dulce chillies, seeded and chopped

1–2 spring onions (scallions), finely chopped

½ small onion, finely chopped

30ml/2 tbsp coriander (cilantro), finely chopped

7.5ml/1½ tsp sugar

5ml/1 tsp salt

5ml/1 tsp finely chopped hot chilli, seeded

1.5ml/¼ tsp black pepper

90ml/6 tbsp oil

Energy 448kcal/1858kJ; Protein 22g; Carbohydrate 4g, of which sugars 3g; Fat 38g, of which saturates 6g; Cholesterol 100mg; Calcium 79mg; Fibre 2.7g; Sodium 799mg

Fried fish with beachfront salad
Pescado frito con ensalada playera

Serves 4

4 whole snapper (each weighing 450–675g/ 1–1½lb), cleaned, scaled and gutted

4 spring onions (scallions), finely chopped

15ml/1 tbsp lime juice

oil for deep-frying

salt and ground black pepper

4 whole limes, quartered, to garnish

coconut rice and patacones, to serve

For the salad

½ onion, thinly sliced

7.5ml/1½ tsp lime juice or white vinegar

30ml/2 tbsp oil

4 large lettuce leaves

4 large tomatoes, sliced

salt and ground black pepper

Fried fish is best eaten at the beach, where little bars serve it with this salad, together with some patacones and coconut rice on the side.

1 Mix the onion for the salad with the lime juice or vinegar, and oil, and season with salt and pepper. Leave for at least 10–20 minutes.

2 Make three or four diagonal cuts down both sides of the fish. Season the inside of each fish with salt and place a quarter of the chopped spring onions in each cavity. Rub salt and pepper over the skin of the fish and sprinkle with lime juice.

3 Heat the oil in a large pan or deep-fat fryer. When it reaches 180°C/350°F, drop in the fish, two at a time, and fry for 15–18 minutes, turning once. Remove from the oil and drain on kitchen paper. Fry the remaining fish.

4 Place a lettuce leaf on each serving plate, add a sliced tomato and some seasoned onion, together with a fish. Garnish with lime wedges, and serve with coconut rice and patacones.

Energy 440kcal/1848kJ; Protein 60g; Carbohydrate 7g, of which sugars 6g; Fat 19g, of which saturates 3g; Cholesterol 111mg; Calcium 140mg; Fibre 1.9g; Sodium 246mg

Fish widow
Viuda de pescado

This dish gets its strange name from a legend about a fisherman's wife who died of a broken heart when her husband betrayed her: her ghost would haunt him at night, dressed as a bride and smelling of fish. It can be prepared with fresh or dried fish. Colombians traditionally use a river fish called bocachico. In some places it is still cooked in clay pots, and it's great for an evening on the beach with everyone sitting around the fire and eating out of coconut cups.

1 Pour the olive oil into a large pan, and tilt it from side to side, so that the bottom and sides of the pan are coated in a thin layer of oil.

2 Arrange the peeled green plantain chunks and the cassava in the base of the pan. On top of the plantain, lay the pieces of yam, pumpkin and potatoes.

3 Pour 120ml/4fl oz/½ cup Tomato and Onion Sauce over the vegetables, and add the coriander and cumin. Then pour over the coconut milk and stock. The liquid should not completely cover the vegetables. Season with salt and pepper then arrange the fish on top.

4 Place the pan over medium heat and bring to the boil, then lower the heat and simmer, covered, for 50 minutes. The fish should cook in the fragrant steam.

5 Meanwhile, bring a smaller pan of water to the boil and drop in the chunks of unpeeled ripe plantain. Cover and simmer for 25 minutes, then drain the plantain and keep warm until the fish is ready.

6 To serve, place a piece or two of each vegetable on each plate. Set a piece of fish on top, add some of the cooking liquid and 30ml/2 tbsp of Tomato and Onion Sauce to each. Serve with the boiled plantain and some boiled white rice.

Serves 4–6

30ml/2 tbsp olive oil

1 small green plantain, peeled, halved and cut into 4cm/1½in chunks

450g/1lb peeled cassava, quartered lengthways and cut into 4cm/1½in chunks

225g/8oz peeled yam, cut into 2.5cm/1in cubes

225g/8oz peeled pumpkin, cut into 2.5cm/1in cubes

225g/8oz sweet potatoes, cut into 2.5cm/1in cubes

1 quantity Tomato and Onion Sauce (see page 39)

5 coriander (cilantro) sprigs

2.5ml/½ tsp ground cumin

475ml/16fl oz/2 cups coconut milk

475ml/16fl oz/2 cups fish stock

6 fillets or steaks of white fish, such as cod, about 2cm/¾in thick (each about 175g/6oz) or 6 whole fish (each about 225g/8oz), soaked overnight if dried

1 small ripe unpeeled plantain, cut into 4cm/1½in chunks

salt and ground black pepper

white rice, to serve

Cook's tip Peel the skin from the plantains before you eat them, as it is not edible. You can do this before serving, if you prefer.

Energy 495kcal/2090kJ; Protein 35g; Carbohydrate 65g, of which sugars 14g; Fat 12g, of which saturates 2g; Cholesterol 81mg; Calcium 98mg; Fibre 4.3g; Sodium 633mg

Creole beef
Bistec a la criolla

Restaurants grill steaks this way over hot coals, but you can use a griddle at home. The chefs relax the beef by slicing it thinly or butterflying it, but I prefer to use thinly sliced skirt steak that has been well aged for this dish. You can prepare it quickly this way and it's a very flavourful cut of meat.

Serves 4–6

675g/1½lb beef skirt (flank) steak, thinly sliced across the grain

15ml/1 tbsp finely chopped coriander (cilantro)

1 garlic clove, finely chopped

1.5ml/¼ tsp cumin

15ml/1 tbsp olive oil

salt and ground black pepper

For the Creole sauce

30ml/2 tbsp oil

1 onion, sliced

2 tomatoes, peeled and sliced

2 garlic cloves, finely chopped

2 ají dulce chillies finely chopped, or 30ml/2 tbsp chopped red (bell) pepper

2 bay leaves

10ml/2 tsp Worcestershire sauce

5ml/1 tsp salt

2.5ml/½ tsp ground black pepper

1 First prepare the Creole sauce. Heat the oil in a large frying pan, then add the sliced onion and tomatoes, together with the chopped garlic and chillies. Stir-fry for 2–3 minutes over a medium to high heat.

2 Add the bay leaves and Worcestershire sauce to the pan, together with the salt and pepper, and cook for a further 5–7 minutes, stirring, until the onions are translucent. The mixture should be thickened, and have the consistency of a sauce. Remove and discard the bay leaves, and keep the sauce warm.

3 Place the thinly sliced beef in a non-metal container. Prepare the charcoal grill if using.

4 In a small bowl, stir the coriander, garlic and cumin into the olive oil, add plenty of black pepper, then use your fingers to rub the mixture over the beef. Cover and set aside for 10 minutes, or until the charcoal is ready.

5 Place the meat on a hot griddle or frying pan. Cook for 2 minutes on each side for rare, 3 minutes for medium, and 4 for well done.

6 Remove the meat from the griddle on to a serving platter or individual plates. Sprinkle with salt, then pour the sauce over the meat. Serve with arepas or warmed flat breads.

Cook's tip There is a world of difference between ready-ground cumin and cumin seeds. Try to use the whole seeds and roast and grind them yourself. Place the seeds in a small, dry pan over medium heat and swirl the pan for 20–30 seconds. The aroma is just divine. Then grind in a mortar and pestle.

Energy 241kcal/1005kJ; Protein 25g; Carbohydrate 4g, of which sugars 3g; Fat 14g, of which saturates 4g; Cholesterol 71mg; Calcium 21mg; Fibre 0.7g; Sodium 424mg

Black beef
Posta negra

Serves 4

2 medium onions, grated

3 thyme sprigs

2 garlic cloves, crushed

15ml/1 tbsp mustard

pinch of ground cloves

900g/2lb beef topside (pot roast)

30ml/2 tbsp oil

120ml/4fl oz/½ cup red wine

250ml/8fl oz/1 cup beef stock

45ml/3 tbsp dark brown sugar

30ml/2 tbsp Worcestershire sauce

salt and ground black pepper

Posta negra is beef that is seasoned, browned and roasted, served with a black sauce made with the pan drippings. At its best when cooked medium-rare and very thinly sliced across the grain, it is delicious in sandwiches.

1 Mix the onions with the thyme, garlic, mustard, cloves and black pepper. Rub over the meat. Set aside for at least 1 hour, or overnight, in the refrigerator. You can leave it for up to 4 days to improve the flavour and tenderness.

2 Remove the meat from the refrigerator 30 minutes before cooking. Preheat the oven to 220°C/425°F/Gas 7.

3 Heat the oil in a pan over medium heat and brown the meat on all sides. Lift the meat out of the pan and transfer to a roasting pan.

4 Roast the meat in the oven for 30–35 minutes, or until a meat thermometer shows an internal temperature of 60°C/140°F. When the meat is done, transfer to a warmed serving dish to rest, covered with foil, for 15–20 minutes.

5 Meanwhile, pour off the fat from the pan. Add the wine to the pan to deglaze, then add the stock, sugar, Worcestershire sauce and salt. Simmer for 5 minutes and set aside.

6 Add any juices from the roasting pan to the sauce, carve the beef and serve with the sauce.

Energy 429kcal/1805kJ; Protein 53g; Carbohydrate 19g, of which sugars 17g; Fat 14g, of which saturates 4g; Cholesterol 113mg; Calcium 59mg; Fibre 1.1g; Sodium 556mg

Baked pork
Cañón de cerdo

A loin of pork is known as a cañón, (tube), in some parts of Colombia. When cooked in this way the pork is usually sweetened with panela or papelón, a concentrated form of raw cane sugar, but brown sugar is used in this recipe.

1 Mix the onion with the brown sugar, garlic, mustard, thyme, oregano, lime rind and juice, and rub all over the pork. Set aside for 1 hour at room temperature or, if possible, overnight in the refrigerator.

2 Preheat the oven to 150°C/300°F/Gas 2. Place the meat on a rack over a roasting pan and sprinkle with salt. Add the beer to the pan.

3 Cook the pork for 1¼ hours, or until the internal temperature of the meat reaches 65°C/150°F. Transfer the pork to warmed serving dish and set aside to rest, covered with foil, for at least 10 minutes.

4 Pour the stock into the roasting pan to deglaze. Heat. stirring in any bits sticking to the bottom. Serve the hot sauce with the meat.

Serves 4–6

1 medium onion, grated

50g/2oz/¼ cup brown sugar

2 garlic cloves, crushed

15ml/1 tbsp mustard

15ml/1 tbsp fresh thyme

15ml/1 tbsp fresh oregano

5ml/1 tsp grated lime rind

15ml/1 tbsp lime juice

1.2kg/2½lb pork loin

5ml/1 tsp salt

350ml/12fl oz/1½ cups light beer

120ml/4fl oz/½ cup stock

Energy 313kcal/1316kJ; Protein 44g; Carbohydrate 13g, of which sugars 12g; Fat 9g, of which saturates 3g; Cholesterol 126mg; Calcium 37mg; Fibre 0.4g; Sodium 530mg

Roast leg of pork
Pernil de cerdo

Leg of pork is a classic festive dish. It serves lots of people and is very simple to cook, and it is beautiful to serve. Buy a boned joint if you prefer, but make sure it has a good 1cm/½in layer of fat on it and leave the skin on, as it makes wonderfully crunchy crackling. Cooking the joint slowly this way produces meat that just falls off the bone. You can leave it in the oven and completely forget about it, then come back to a tender and delicious dish.

1 Make deep crisscross cuts 2.5cm/1in apart all over the skin of the pork. A craft knife or scalpel with a new blade is useful for this.

2 Mix the grated onions with the garlic, mustard, thyme, Worcestershire sauce, 5ml/1 tsp salt, 10ml/2 tsp pepper and the cloves. Rub this all over the meat and chill for 24 hours.

3 Remove the pork from the refrigerator, and bring to room temperature for about 1½ hours.

4 Preheat the oven to 110°C/ 225°F/Gas ¼. Place all the ingredients for the glaze in a small pan. Bring to the boil and simmer for 7–8 minutes or until slightly thickened, then remove from the heat.

5 Place the pork in a roasting pan. Spread or brush a quarter of the glaze over the joint. Add the beer to the pan. Cook in the oven for 30 minutes per 450g/1lb, or until a meat thermometer shows an internal temperature of 70–80°C/160–180°F. Let the meat rest for 30 minutes before carving.

6 To prepare the sauce, scrape all the meat juices and drippings from the roasting pan, pass through a sieve and skim off the fat. Add the juices to the remaining glaze, stir in the flour and cook until thickened.

Variation A lightly smoked leg is also delicious cooked this way. You can peel or cut off the thick skin in minutes, and cut the fat into squares as in step 1.

Serves 10–12

1 leg of pork with bone (about 3.5–4.5kg/8–10lb)

2 medium onions, grated

4 garlic cloves, finely chopped

120ml/4fl oz/½ cup mustard

30ml/2 tbsp fresh thyme

30ml/2 tbsp Worcestershire sauce

30ml/2 tbsp salt

7.5ml/1½ tsp black pepper

2.5ml/½ tsp ground cloves

350ml/12fl oz/1½ cups light beer

7.5ml/1½ tsp flour

For the glaze

175g/6 oz/¾ cup dark brown sugar

250ml/8fl oz/1 cup red wine

250ml/8fl oz/1 cup vegetable stock

50g/2 oz/¼ cup Dijon mustard

60ml/4 tbsp dried thyme

zest of 1 orange, grated

10ml/2 tsp pepper

5ml/1 tsp salt

Energy 455kcal/1916kJ; Protein 73g; Carbohydrate 19g, of which sugars 18g; Fat 8g, of which saturates 2g; Cholesterol 213mg; Calcium 66mg; Fibre 0.4g; Sodium 1582mg

Antioqueño platter
Bandeja Paisa

This is one of Colombia's most popular main dishes. Not many people can get through such a huge amount of food, yet it is eaten daily in the higher Andean zone, where the difficult terrain means farmers have to work hard and they get really hungry. The cool mountain weather gives everyone the appetite of a tiger, then after a meal like this a long siesta follows.

Serves 4–6

3–5 tbsp oil, plus extra for frying the plantains

6 chorizos, 10cm/4in long

2 very ripe plantains

4–6 eggs

600g/1lb 6oz/4 cups cooked white rice and 1 quantity Chicharrones (*see* page 37), to serve

For the Antioqueño beans

225g/8 oz/1¼ cups dried cargamanto, red kidney or pinto beans

225g/8 oz slab of bacon, cut into 5mm/¼ in dice

1 quantity Tomato and Onion Sauce (*see* page 39)

For the ground beef

675g/1½lb beef skirt steak, cut into 5cm/2in strips

1 medium onion, grated

1 garlic clove, finely chopped

1.5ml/¼ tsp salt

1.5ml/¼ tsp ground cumin

1 To make the Antioqueño beans, place the dried beans in a bowl with 1.5 litres/2½ pints/6¼ cups water and leave to soak overnight.

2 The next day, drain the beans and place in a pan with the bacon and 1 litre/1¾ pints/4 cups of water (fresh or from the soaking water).

3 Bring to the boil and simmer for 2½ hours, or until tender but not too soft. (Alternatively, cook them in a pressure cooker for 45 minutes.)

4 While the beans are cooking, prepare the beef. Place the meat, onion and garlic in a large pan and add 1.5 litres/2½ pints/6 cups water. Bring to the boil, then lower the heat and simmer, covered, for 1½ hours, until very tender.

5 Strain, reserving the stock for another use. Set the meat aside until cool enough to handle, then transfer to a food processor, add the salt and cumin, and grind until almost powdered.

6 Add the Tomato and Onion Sauce to the beans and cook uncovered for 30 minutes, until the liquid is reduced to a velvety sauce.

7 Heat half the oil in a pan and shallow fry the chorizos until browned. Keep warm.

8 To make the sweet plantain slices, peel the plantains by cutting the ends off and then slitting down one side and pulling back the skin from this cut. Slice the plantains diagonally into 5mm/¼ in slices.

9 Pour a 5cm/2in depth of oil into a large, wide pan and heat it to 180°C/350°F. Fry the slices for 2–3 minutes on each side, until they turn dark orange. Lift them out with a slotted spoon and drain on kitchen paper. Keep warm.

10 Just before you are ready to serve, heat some oil in a frying pan and fry the eggs. Reheat the beef if necessary.

11 To assemble each platter, arrange a portion of cooked rice at one end and beans at the other. Between the rice and beans, arrange a portion of beef on one side and a chorizo on the other. Lay some plantain slices over the beef, a fried egg on top of the rice and a chicharron over the beans.

Energy 937kcal/3918kJ; Protein 55g; Carbohydrate 65g, of which sugars 10g; Fat 53g, of which saturates 15g; Cholesterol 323mg; Calcium 105mg; Fibre 4.7g; Sodium 1291mg

Chicken Casserole
Pollo sudado

This dish is prepared in many Colombian and Venezuelan homes at least once a week. It is usually cooked in a pan on the stove like soup, and served with white rice. Potatoes are added to extend the dish and make it feed more people; they take on a unique and delicious flavour and are eaten first.

1 Mix the grated onion, crushed garlic and Worcestershire sauce in a small bowl, and season with 5ml/1 tsp salt and some pepper. Rub the mixture on to the chicken pieces and set aside for 10 minutes.

2 Heat the oil in a large pan and brown the chicken pieces over medium heat for 5–7 minutes. Remove the chicken from the pan and pour off the excess fat.

3 Pour in the stock and stir to deglaze the pan. Add the tomatoes, potatoes and achiote or turmeric and season with salt. Return the chicken to the pan and simmer, covered, for 50 minutes, or until the chicken is tender and the potatoes are cooked through.

4 Remove the lid and cook for 15 minutes more to reduce the cooking liquid to almost nothing before serving with white rice.

Serves 4–6

1 medium onion, grated

3 garlic cloves, crushed

25ml/1½ tbsp Worcestershire sauce

12 chicken legs, with skin

6 chicken wings

15ml/1 tbsp oil

475ml/16fl oz/2 cups chicken stock

475ml/16fl oz/2 cups chopped tomatoes

675g/1½lb small red potatoes, peeled and quartered

5ml/1 tsp achiote or turmeric

salt and ground black pepper

cooked white rice, to serve

Cook's tip You must use waxy, not floury, potatoes for this dish, as they won't disintegrate during cooking.

Energy 355kcal/1485kJ; Protein 25g; Carbohydrate 24g, of which sugars 4g; Fat 18g, of which saturates 5g; Cholesterol 128mg; Calcium 31mg; Fibre 2.4g; Sodium 133mg

Garlic chicken
Pollo asado

Serves 4

1 whole chicken, about
1kg/2¼lb in weight

1 lime quartered

2–3 spring onions (scallions),
chopped

15ml/1 tbsp butter

2–3 garlic cloves, chopped

2.5ml/½ tsp ground cumin

5ml/1 tsp salt

1.5ml/¼ tsp ground black
pepper

15ml/1 tbsp Worcestershire
sauce

white rice, to serve

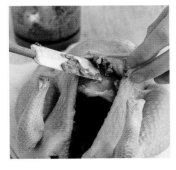

Grilled chicken joints are popular in asaderos – restaurants with huge charcoal grills where Colombian families love to eat at weekends. At home it is more convenient to roast a whole chicken in the oven and joint it at the table, but you can still use the same delicious flavourings. Serve with white rice and perhaps a tomato salad.

1 Wash and dry the chicken and rub it inside and out with the lime quarters.

2 Put the spring onions into a blender or food processor with the butter, garlic, cumin, salt, pepper and Worcestershire sauce. Process to a paste. Ease the chicken skin away from the breast and push the paste under the skin.

3 Leave the chicken to absorb the flavours for at least 1 hour, or preferably overnight, in the refrigerator. About 30 minutes before cooking, remove the chicken from the refrigerator.

4 Preheat the oven to 200°C/400°F/Gas 6. Roast the chicken for 1½ hours, then slice or cut into pieces and serve with white rice.

Energy 285kcal/1187kJ; Protein 28g; Carbohydrate 2g, of which sugars 1g; Fat 18g, of which saturates 6g; Cholesterol 132mg; Calcium 36mg; Fibre 0.2g; Sodium 672mg

Baked lamb
Asado de cordero

This traditional dish is one for special occasions such as birthdays or family gatherings. When it is prepared on farms that raise their own animals, a very young lamb is chosen, and wild blueberries are picked to make a preserve. Freshly cooked arepas are the usual accompaniment to the fragrant meat.

1 Lay the lamb in a close-fitting dish and pour the milk over it. Leave it to soak for 4 hours to sweeten the flavour, turning the meat over halfway through.

2 Lift out the lamb and dry it with kitchen paper. Discard the milk and return the lamb to the rinsed-out dish.

3 Mix the onions, lime juice, garlic, oregano, bay leaf, salt, pepper and cumin in a small bowl, and rub the mixture over the lamb. Leave overnight in the refrigerator to absorb the flavours.

4 Preheat the oven to 180°C/350°F/Gas 4. Place the lamb on a rack over a roasting pan and pour 120ml/4fl oz/½ cup of the stock into the pan with the beer and the sugar. Place the meat in the preheated oven.

5 After 1 hour, check the liquid in the pan. If it has reduced to almost nothing and the drippings are browning, add a little extra stock. Cook for a further 30 minutes. When the cooking time is over, or a meat thermometer reads 55°C/130°F, remove from the oven.

6 Transfer the meat to a warmed serving dish and leave to rest, covered, for 10 minutes.

7 Pour any remaining stock into the pan and stir over a low heat to deglaze it. Pass through a sieve into a bowl (reserving the contents of the sieve) and skim off the fat.

8 Pour the skimmed gravy into a small pan and add the blueberry preserve and the sieved seasonings, stir to mix, then bring to the boil, stirring. Cut the lamb into generous slices, and serve with the sauce.

Serves 4–6

1.8kg/4lb leg of lamb, on the bone

750ml/1¼ pints/3 cups milk

2 medium onions, grated

30ml/2 tbsp lime juice

3 garlic cloves, crushed

15ml/1 tbsp dried oregano

1 bay leaf, crumbled

7.5ml/1½ tsp salt

1.5ml/¼ tsp pepper

1.5ml/¼ tsp ground cumin

350ml/12fl oz/1½ cups stock

350ml/12fl oz/1½ cups light beer

5ml/1 tsp sugar

115g/4oz blueberry preserve

fresh arepas, to serve (see page 29)

Cook's tip You can also use butterflied leg of lamb for this dish. Roast at 200°C/400°F/Gas 6 for 50 minutes to 1 hour.

Energy 256kcal/2196kJ; Protein 43g; Carbohydrate 26g, of which sugars 24g; Fat 27g, of which saturates 12g; Cholesterol 163mg; Calcium 193mg; Fibre 0.8g; Sodium 836mg

Venezuelan platter
Pabellón

Serves 8

For the black beans

225g/8 oz/2 cups black beans, soaked overnight in 1.5 litres/2½ pints/6¼ cups water

1 pig's trotter

½ onion

¼ red pepper

30ml/2 tbsp dark brown sugar

1 quantity Tomato and Onion Sauce (see page 39)

For the pulled beef

675g/1½lb beef skirt (flank) steak, cut into strips

1 onion, grated

30ml/2 tbsp oil

1.5ml/¼ tsp achiote or turmeric

5 spring onions (scallions), finely chopped

3 tomatoes, peeled, seeded and diced

3 garlic cloves, finely chopped

1.5ml/¼ tsp salt

1.5ml/¼ tsp ground cumin

For the white rice

15ml/1 tbsp oil

1 spring onion (scallion), finely chopped

1 garlic clove, crushed

5ml/1 tsp finely chopped aji dulce chilli

275g/9oz/1½ cups white long grain rice

5ml/1 tsp salt

For the fried sweet plantains

2 very ripe plantains

475ml/16fl oz/2 cups oil, for frying

This is Venezuela's signature dish. It's a hearty feast that includes the four favourite foods of this wonderful Caribbean country: black beans, carne mechada, or 'pulled' beef, white rice and fried sweet plantains.

1 Drain the beans and put them in a pan with the pig's trotter, onions, red pepper and 1.5 litre/2½ pints/6 cups fresh water. Bring to the boil and simmer for 2½ hours, until tender.

2 Remove the pig's trotter from the pan, and add the brown sugar and Tomato and Onion Sauce to the beans. Cook, uncovered, for a further 30 minutes, until the sauce is velvety.

3 While the beans are cooking, prepare the pulled beef. Place the meat and onion in a large pan and add 1.5 litres/2½ pints/6¼ cups water. Bring to the boil then lower the heat and simmer, covered, for 1½ hours, until tender.

4 Strain and reserve the stock, and set the meat aside. When cool enough, use your fingers to separate the meat into thin fibres.

5 Return the pan to the heat and add the oil, achiote and spring onions. Cook for 2 minutes, then stir in the tomatoes, garlic, salt and cumin. Add the shredded beef with 250ml/8fl oz/1 cup of the beef stock and cook for 15 minutes, until the sauce is reduced. Set aside.

6 Now prepare the rice. Heat the oil in a pan over medium-high heat and sauté the spring onion, garlic and chilli for 1 minute. Pour in the rice and salt and cook for another minute, stirring. Add 750ml/1¼ pints/3 cups water and bring to the boil. When the rice is jumping near the surface of the water, reduce the heat, cover the pan and cook gently for 20 minutes.

7 To prepare the sweet plantain slices, peel the plantains by cutting the ends off and then slitting down one side and pulling back the skin from this cut. Slice the plantains diagonally into 5mm/¼in slices.

8 Pour a 5cm/2in depth of oil into a large, wide pan and heat it to 180°C/350°F. Fry the plantain slices for 2–3 minutes on each side, until they turn dark orange.

9 Lift the plantains out with a slotted spoon and drain on kitchen paper.

10 Reheat the pulled beef and black beans if necessary, and serve together with the rice and fried plantains.

Energy 517kcal/2176kJ; Protein 28g; Carbohydrate 59g, of which sugars 11g; Fat 20g, of which saturates 4g; Cholesterol 46mg; Calcium 80mg; Fibre 1.7g; Sodium 376mg

Venezuelan corn wraps
Hayacas

Traditionally eaten at Christmas, these plantain-leaf wrapped cakes are labour intensive but make a special treat for family parties.

1 Process the onion, red pepper, garlic, tomatoes, cumin, salt and pepper and transfer to a large bowl. Add the pork and chicken, and mix, then set aside for 10 minutes.

2 Heat the oil in a large pan over medium heat and cook the meat, for 10 minutes, stirring. Add 1.5 litres/2½ pints/6¼ cups water, bring to the boil, then lower the heat, cover and cook for 30 minutes. Strain off and reserve the stock. Remove the chicken meat from the bones and dice. Mix the meats with the Tomato and Onion Sauce and set aside to cool.

3 For the wraps, remove the centre vein from the plaintain leaves. Pass each half leaf over a burner on your stove until darkened: this makes the leaves easier to work with. Cut the plantain leaves into 40 x 30cm/12in squares.

4 To make the masa, dissolve the brown sugar in 250ml/8fl oz/1 cup water in a large pan. Add the cornmeal, Tomato and Onion Sauce, stock, fat or oil, and achiote and beat together Place the pan over medium-low heat and cook for 5 minutes, beating with a wooden spoon, until thick. Turn on to a work surface and knead for 1 minute, until smooth. Divide into 20 balls.

5 To assemble the wraps, brush one side of each plantain square with oil. Add a ball of dough and flatten to a 15cm/6in circle, roughly 5mm/¼in thick. Place a piece of pork and chicken on top, add some sauce, then 1 tomato slice, 2 onion slices, 2 olives, 2 capers, 5 raisins and 30ml/2 tbsp reserved stock.

6 Bring two sides of the leaf together so that the masa is folded around the filling. Fold over the edges of the leaf and flatten the parcel, then fold in the remaining two sides. Turn over and place in the centre of another oiled leaf. Fold over the sides in the same way and tie the parcel with twine. Repeat to make 20 wraps.

7 Half-fill a large pan (preferably a stock pan with a pierced insert) with water, add 15ml/ 1 tbsp salt and bring to the boil. When the water is boiling strongly, place the parcels in the insert and weight them with a plate or pan lid so that they do not float. Cover the pan and simmer for 1 hour. After 45 minutes, check that all the parcels are still submerged and top up with boiling water if necessary.

8 To serve, pile the parcels on a serving platter for each person to unwrap at the table.

Serves 8–10

For the filling

2 onions

1 red (bell) pepper

6 garlic cloves

2 large tomatoes

5ml/1 tsp ground cumin

10ml/2 tsp salt

1.5ml/¼ tsp pepper

900g/2lb meaty pork ribs, cut into 1cm/½in chunks

1 large or 2 small chickens (1.8–2.25kg/4–5lb total weight), jointed

30ml/2 tbsp oil

150ml/5 fl oz/1¼ cups Tomato and Onion Sauce (see page 39)

For the masa

50g/2oz/¼ cup dark brown sugar

200g/7oz/2 cups pre-cooked yellow cornmeal

50ml/2fl oz/¼ cup Tomato and Onion Sauce

550ml/18fl oz/2½ cups stock (from cooking the chicken and pork)

45ml/3 tbsp pork fat or oil

5ml/1 tsp achiote or turmeric

To assemble the wraps

about 3 whole plantain or banana leaves, washed

50ml/2fl oz/¼ cup oil

4 tomatoes, sliced

2 onions, sliced

40 green olives, sliced

45–60ml/3–4 tbsp capers

75–115g/3–4oz/½–⅔ cup raisins

Energy 570kcal/2382kJ; Protein 36g; Carbohydrate 35g, of which sugars 19g; Fat 33g, of which saturates 8g; Cholesterol 123mg; Calcium 60mg; Fibre 2.6g; Sodium 1006mg

Rice Dishes

Rice is another staple ingredient that is eaten daily, either as a side dish alongside meat and fish, or as the basis for a main course.

Regional favourites and national dishes

White rice is prepared every day as a side dish along with a second side dish of plantain, yucca, potato and other roots and tubers. In restaurants it is served in a little dome, formed in a cup and turned out onto the plate, often decorated with chopped green spring onions (scallions) or a subtle herb such as chervil. A traditional rice dish from the Caribbean region is arroz con coco (coconut rice), which is prepared slightly differently depending on the locality. This is always served with freshly fried fish and accompanied by patacones (plantain fritters) and salad, especially in beachside restaurants. This kind of rice and fish mixture brings back memories of happy holidays at the seaside to most Colombians and Venezuelans.

Rice can also be simmered with vegetables such as red (bell) peppers, onions, lentils and many others, but most cooks add only one extra vegetable per dish so that a certain amount of colour and flavour is added to the basic rice but the dish does not overpower the main course.

Rice is also a staple ingredient that is combined with many other flavoursome ingredients such as poultry to make one-dish meals such as arroz con pollo (chicken and rice) or arroz atollado, the Colombian form of moist, spiced and deliciously aromatic risotto. When rice is the basis for a main course it is usually served with fried sweet plantains or platanitos (green plantain chips).

Right middle: A traditional horse and carriage in the historic quarter of Cartagena, Colombia.
Page 83: A typical colonial-style house in Barichara, Colombia.

White coconut rice
Arroz con coco blanco

This simple rice dish, with its distinctive and unusual sweetness, is eaten mostly in the coastal areas of Colombia, and especially in the old city of Cartagena de Indias, the port of arrival for the Spanish conquistadors. It is served with patacones, lime slices and salad, and can also accompany traditional foods such as black beef or fried fish and other seafood recipes, including soups.

Serves 4–6

1 litre/1¾ pints/4 cups fresh coconut milk, or 475ml/16fl oz/2 cups canned coconut milk mixed with 350ml/12fl oz/1½ cups water, or 1 large fresh coconut

45ml/3 tbsp dark brown sugar

300g/11oz/1½ cups rice

15ml/3 tsp salt

lime wedges, to serve

Cook's tip You can prepare coconut milk in advance and store it in the refrigerator for up to 3 days, or freeze it for up to 6 months, keeping the two pressings separate. When you buy a coconut, shake it to check there is plenty of liquid inside.

1 If using fresh coconut, make the coconut milk. There are three spots in the end of the coconut, one of which is softer than the others. Pierce this and invert the coconut over a bowl to catch the water.

2 Once it has drained, smash the coconut with a hammer and prise off the white flesh from the inside of the shell with the tip of a strong knife. Remove any brown skin with a knife or a potato peeler. Finely shred or grate the flesh.

3 Put the grated coconut in a blender or food processor with the coconut water and about 250ml/8fl oz/1 cup of hot water. Blend for 1 minute, then pour into a muslin (cheesecloth)-lined colander over a bowl. Press with a spoon to extract all the milk; this is the first pressing.

4 Return the coconut to the blender and blend with another 475ml/16fl oz/2 cups hot water. Press through the muslin in the same way as before, but drain the milk into a separate bowl. This makes the second pressing. Discard the coconut flesh.

5 You are now ready to make the rice. Put the milk from the first pressing, if using milk from fresh coconuts, or 350ml/12fl oz/1½ cups canned coconut milk, in a pan.

6 Add the sugar and cook over medium high heat for 20 minutes, until the milk has thickened to a paste-like consistency.

7 Add the coconut milk from the second pressing, or the remaining milk from the can, and the water, and mix with the thick paste until smoothly blended.

8 Add the rice and salt to the pan, and stir thoroughly. Simmer the rice for 7 minutes, or until the grains appear at the surface and the steam is making circular holes as it bubbles out of the mixture.

9 Reduce the heat to a minimum, cover the pan and cook for 20 minutes, until the milk is completely absorbed and the rice is tender. Fluff up the rice with a fork, then serve straight away with wedges of lime.

Energy 258kcal/1099kJ; Protein 4g; Carbohydrate 59g, of which sugars 16g; Fat 2g, of which saturates 1g; Cholesterol 0mg; Calcium 75mg; Fibre 0.2g; Sodium 1168mg

Crab and coconut risotto
Arroz de cangrejo y coco

Serves 4–6

15ml/1 tbsp salt

15ml/1 tbsp crab boil seasoning (see Cook's tip)

4–6 crabs

1 quantity Tomato and Onion Sauce (*see* page 39)

600g/1lb 6oz/3 cups long grain rice

3 culantro leaves or coriander (cilantro) sprig, chopped

475g/16fl oz/2 cups coconut milk

Cook's tip To make crab boil seasoning, mix together 60ml/4 tbsp yellow mustard seeds, 45ml/3 tbsp coriander seeds, 30ml/2 tbsp each of allspice berries and dill seeds, 15ml/1 tbsp each of crushed chilli, black peppercorns and whole cloves, and 8 bay leaves. Store in an airtight container.

This light, creamy concoction of crab and coconut milk is very popular on the Pacific coast. To kill a crab or lobster quickly and humanely, hold it belly up on a board. Quickly push a large, sharp knife into the head between the eyes.

1 Put 2 litres/3½ pints/8 cups of water into a large pan, add the salt and seasoning and bring to the boil over high heat. Wrap the crab boil seasoning in a square of muslin (cheesecloth), tie securely and drop into the cooking water.

2 Add the crabs, boil for 5–7 minutes, then lift them out and set aside. When cool enough to handle, cut the crabs in half, remove the meat and set aside. Return the shells to the stock to add extra flavour.

3 Boil the stock until it has reduced to about 1 litre/1¾ pints/4 cups. Strain and set aside.

4 Set a pan over medium heat and add the Tomato and Onion Sauce, the rice and culantro or coriander. Sauté, stirring, for 2 minutes, then add the coconut milk and crab stock.

5 Reduce the heat to low and simmer, covered, for 30 minutes, until the rice is tender. Stir in the crab meat and serve immediately.

Energy 556kcal/2351kJ; Protein 22g; Carbohydrate 94g, of which sugars 7g; Fat 13g, of which saturates 2g; Cholesterol 50mg; Calcium 90mg; Fibre 1.3g; Sodium 1573mg

Rice with prawns
Arroz de camarón

This Caribbean recipe is traditionally prepared with dried shrimp, although fresh shellfish can also be used. It is popular in the old coastal city of Santa Marta, where the banana trade attracted foreigners, including my Scottish great-grandfather, to captain boats up the Magdalena River. The dish is often served with patacones.

1 Peel the prawns, reserving the meat. Put the heads and shells in a pan with 2 litres/3½ pints/8 cups water. Add the coriander, onion and pepper, cover and bring to the boil. Reduce the heat and simmer for 15 minutes. Pour the contents of the pan into a food processor and blend together, then pass the stock through a fine sieve and set aside.

2 Heat the oil in a pan and add the grated pepper, carrot, spring onions, chillies and achiote. Cover and cook for 5 minutes.

3 Stir the garlic, tomatoes, salt and pepper into the pan, and cook, uncovered, for a further 5 minutes, stirring from time to time.

4 Add the shelled prawns to the pan, with the rice and 1.5 litres/2½ pints/6¼ cups of the reserved stock. Bring slowly to a simmer, then cover the pan, lower the heat to minimum and cook for 20 minutes.

5 Once the rice is cooked, serve it with sweet plantain fritters.

Serves 4–6

1.2kg/2½lb large raw prawns (shrimp)

4 coriander (cilantro) sprigs

½ onion

½ red (bell) pepper

30ml/2 tbsp oil

1 red (bell) pepper, grated

1 carrot, grated

2 spring onions (scallions), finely chopped

3 green ají dulce chillies, finely chopped

2.5ml/½ tsp achiote or turmeric

3–4 garlic cloves, crushed

2 medium tomatoes, peeled, seeded and diced

15ml/1 tbsp salt

2.5ml/½ tsp black pepper

600g/1lb 6oz/3 cups long grain rice

Plantain fritters, to serve (see page 101)

Energy 502kcal/2134kJ; Protein 25g; Carbohydrate 90g, of which sugars 4g; Fat 7g, of which saturates 1g; Cholesterol 210mg; Calcium 150mg; Fibre 1.5g; Sodium 2194mg

Chicken and rice
Arroz con pollo

Serves 8–10

For the chicken and stock

4 chicken breast portions on the bone

450g/1lb chicken wings

2 medium onions, grated

1 carrot, grated

1 red (bell) pepper, grated

10 coriander (cilantro) sprigs

6 garlic cloves, crushed

15ml/1 tbsp achiote or turmeric

2.5ml/½ tsp black peppercorns

For the rice

30ml/2 tbsp oil

3 medium onions, cut into 5mm/¼ in dice

3 carrots, cut into 5mm/¼ in dice

225g/8 oz/1½ cups green beans, cut into 5mm/¼ in dice

115g/4oz/1 cup fresh peas

45ml/3 tbsp finely chopped coriander (cilantro)

90ml/6 tbsp tomato purée (paste)

30ml/2 tbsp soy sauce

30ml/2 tbsp Worcestershire sauce

15ml/1 tbsp finely chopped garlic

15ml/1 tbsp sugar

1.5ml/¼ tsp achiote or turmeric

12.5ml/2½ tsp salt

1.5ml/¼ tsp ground black pepper

400g/14oz/2 cups long grain white rice

This is a favourite dish all over Colombia and Venezuela. It's one that many families prepare on Saturday, when they have time to linger at the table and enjoy each other's company over a great one-dish meal. The fanciest versions are made with all white chicken meat, but where money is an issue the dish is made using giblets and wings. All versions are delicious to eat with a salad and some fried plantains.

1 Place the chicken breasts and wings in a large pan with 2.4 litres/4 pints/10 cups water and add the onions, carrot, grated red pepper, coriander sprigs, garlic, achiote and peppercorns. Bring to the boil, then reduce the heat and simmer, covered, for 15 minutes.

2 Remove the chicken from the pan, strip off the meat and set aside. Put the bones back in the stock and leave to simmer, uncovered, to reduce the liquid to 1 litre/1¾ pints/4 cups. Strain and reserve. Cut the meat into bitesize chunks or strips.

3 For the rice, heat the oil in a pan over medium heat. Add the onions, carrots, green beans, and peas and sauté for 2 minutes.

4 Add the coriander, tomato purée and soy sauce to the pan, with the Worcestershire sauce, garlic, sugar, achiote or turmeric, 2.5ml/½ tsp salt and the pepper. Continue to cook over medium heat for 4 minutes, until all the vegetables are al dente.

5 Add the rice to the pan and cook, stirring, for 1 minute to coat it in the oil. Add the stock and the remaining salt and bring to the boil. As soon as you see the rice rising to the surface, cover the pot, reduce the heat to a minimum and cook for 20 minutes.

6 When the rice is tender and the stock absorbed, add the chicken, folding it in with two forks to keep the rice fluffy. Cover and cook for 2 minutes for the chicken to reheat, then serve with fried plantains, and a salad if you wish.

Energy 341kcal/1439kJ; Protein 24g; Carbohydrate 50g, of which sugars 12g; Fat 7g, of which saturates 1g; Cholesterol 53mg; Calcium 78mg; Fibre 3.7g; Sodium 824mg

Pork and chorizo risotto
Arroz atollado

A traditional dish from the Pacific region of Colombia, arroz atollado is usually prepared over log fires in farm-like restaurants that people visit to remember and enjoy traditional recipes they remember from their childhood. The risotto is a strongly flavoured dish, cooked with Tomato and Onion Sauce, garnished with coriander and often served with patacones.

1 Place a large pan over medium-high heat and lightly brown the pork for 5–8 minutes. Pour off and retain the rendered fat.

2 Add 3 litres/5¼ pints/13¼ cups of water to the pork in the pan, together with the onion and spring onions, garlic, culantro or coriander leaves and pepper. Bring to the boil, then lower the heat, cover and simmer for 45 minutes.

3 Pass the stock through a sieve and set aside. Discard the vegetable pieces in the sieve but reserve the pork.

4 Heat the rendered oil or pork fat in a clean pan, add the chorizo and sauté over medium-high heat for 2 minutes, stirring, until browned.

5 Add the cooked pork to the pan, with two-thirds of the Tomato and Onion Sauce, the potatoes, rice, salt, cumin, achiote or turmeric, chilli and 2 litres/3½ pints/8 cups of reserved stock. Stir the ingredients together and bring to the boil, then reduce the heat and simmer, covered, for 30 minutes.

6 When the rice is tender (it should be moist, as in a risotto) and the stock almost absorbed, stir in the vermouth and cook for a further 2 minutes.

7 Serve the rice immediately, topped with some of the remaining Tomato and Onion Sauce and sprinkled with coriander.

Serves 4–6

675g/1½lb meaty pork ribs, cut into 5cm/2in chunks

½ onion

2 spring onions (scallions)

2 garlic cloves

2 culantro leaves or a sprig of coriander

2.5ml/½ tsp ground black pepper

15ml/1 tbsp oil or rendered pork fat

1 chorizo, 15cm/6in long, cut into 5mm/¼in dice

1½ quantities Tomato and Onion Sauce (see page 39)

225g/8oz yellow potatoes, peeled and cut into 1cm/½in dice

250g/9oz/1¼ cups white long grain rice

15ml/1 tbsp salt

2.5ml/½ tsp ground cumin

5ml/1 tsp achiote or turmeric

5ml/1 tsp hot chilli, finely chopped

120ml/4fl oz/½ cup vermouth

60ml/4 tbsp coriander (cilantro), finely chopped

Energy 597kcal/2502kJ; Protein 30g; Carbohydrate 51g, of which sugars 8g; Fat 30g, of which saturates 9g; Cholesterol 77mg; Calcium 73mg; Fibre 2.3g; Sodium 1501mg

Side Dishes

This chapter contains a colourful mixture
of delightful dishes to accompany
main meals or to eat on their own
as a light lunch or supper.

Savoury and sweet side dishes to tempt the taste buds

Main dishes in the hot, steamy coastal Caribbean are generally served with sweet side dishes such as torta de plátano (sweet plantain pie) or enyucado (cassava bread).

Plantain is a real staple in Colombia and Venezuela, and the combination of savoury meat, poultry or fish and sweet plantain is really enjoyed in these tropical areas, reflecting the vivid surroundings. Some of the sweet dishes that would accompany a Caribbean lunch are served as dessert in the colder Andean region, and are also eaten as snacks. Other dishes, such as papas saladas (salted potatoes) are also eaten as appetizers.

Cassava, also known as yuca, is another favourite ingredient, which can be simply steamed or fried, or served with a delicious buttery cheese sauce (yuca guisada). All the common tubers and roots such as potatoes and yuca can be served hot or cold, salty or sweet, as their bland taste absorbs seasonings beautifully. They can also be topped with a sauce or melted cheese. Try these side dishes with your favourite main course, or on their own for a taste of South America.

Page 95: The trail to the Colombian Cuidad Perdida in the Amazonian rainforest.
Right middle: The pretty, 500 year old mountain village of Villa de Leyva, Colombia.

Cassava bread
Enyucado

This is a moist, chewy, delicious cake, made at home all the time as a side dish – and often eaten warm from the oven. It is also sold on the streets as a snack. On the Caribbean coast, people love to mix sweet and savoury ingredients this way.

1 Preheat the oven to 180°C/350°F/Gas 4. Butter a 15 x 20cm/6 x 8in baking tin (pan).

2 Place the cassava in a large bowl and mix in the coconut, cheese, sugar, 30ml/2 tbsp of the melted butter, the ground aniseed and salt.

3 Transfer to the prepared tin, and drizzle the remaining tablespoon of butter over the top.

4 Bake the cake in the oven for 45 minutes, or until a knife comes out clean when inserted into the cake. Cool for 10 minutes, then cut into squares and serve warm.

Cook's tips The cassava will be very watery when grated; this is fine, do not press it. Don't keep this bread in the refrigerator, as it will become too hard.

Serves 8–10

450g/1lb cassava, peeled and finely grated

40g/1½oz/½ cup finely grated fresh coconut

75g/3oz/½ cup finely grated queso blanco (soft white farmer's cheese) or mozzarella

150g/5oz/¾ cup sugar

45ml/3 tbsp melted butter, plus extra for greasing

5ml/1 tsp ground aniseed

1.5ml/¼ tsp salt

Energy 203kcal/853kJ; Protein 2g; Carbohydrate 33g, of which sugars 17g; Fat 8g, of which saturates 6g; Cholesterol 14mg; Calcium 38mg; Fibre 0.7g; Sodium 100mg

Salted potatoes
Papas saladas

Serves 4–6

450g/1lb (about 10) small
  new potatoes

40ml/2½ tbsp salt

Cook's tip These potatoes
are also good as an appetizer,
served with Herb Sauce
(*see* page 38) to dip them
into, or with Tomato and
Onion Sauce (*see* page 39)
poured over the top.

For this simple dish choose uniformly-sized, waxy-fleshed red or yellow potatoes
that are small enough to cook whole. Papas saladas are delicious with grilled meats
or fish, and are so good that you can also eat them at room temperature.

1 Wash the potatoes well. Do not peel or cut
them, and keep the skin intact.

2 Place the potatoes in a pan with water to
barely cover them. Add the salt.

3 Cook, covered, on medium heat, for 30–45
minutes, until all the water has evaporated.

4 Swirl the pan gently so that the salt sticks to
the potatoes, serve straight away.

Energy 53kcal/224kJ; Protein 1g; Carbohydrate 12g, of which sugars 1g; Fat 0g; Cholesterol 0mg; Calcium 5mg; Fibre 0.8g; Sodium 2628mg

Potatoes in creamy sauce
Papas chorreadas

Serves 4–6

450g/1lb small potatoes

30ml/2 tbsp butter

4 spring onions (scallions), shredded

2.5ml/½ tsp finely chopped garlic

2 medium tomatoes, peeled, seeded and diced

1.5ml/¼ tsp ground cumin

120ml/4fl oz/½ cup vegetable stock

175ml/6fl oz/¾ cup single (light) cream

150g/5oz queso blanco or mozzarella, shredded

salt and ground black pepper

Cook's tip Half-peeling the potatoes means that texture is retained, the sauce is absorbed better through the peeled areas.

These delicious potatoes are so flavourful and creamy you could almost eat them as a meal by themselves. They are partially peeled and bathed in a sautéed onion and tomato sauce, thickened with cream and melted cheese.

1 Peel the potatoes in sections, leaving about half the skin on each one, and boil them whole in salted water for 15–20 minutes, or until cooked through.

2 Meanwhile, make the sauce. Place the butter in a pan over medium heat, add the spring onions and cook, covered, for 5 minutes. Stir in the garlic and cook for a few seconds more.

3 Add the tomatoes and cumin to the onions and garlic, season with salt and pepper, cover again and cook for 15 minutes more. Drain the potatoes and keep warm in a serving dish.

4 Add the stock, cream and cheese to the sauce and cook, uncovered, for 3–4 minutes, until the cheese has melted. Pour the sauce over the potatoes, and serve.

Energy 217kcal/903kJ; Protein 7g; Carbohydrate 14g, of which sugars 3g; Fat 15g, of which saturates 10g; Cholesterol 41mg; Calcium 127mg; Fibre 1.1g; Sodium 204mg

Plantain fritters
Patacones

Every household in Colombia eats these at least once a week! As well as making them with totally green plantains, I also make them with plantains that have a hint of yellow in their skin so they are a little sweet; these need to be cooked for a shorter time and at a lower temperature. Patacones also work wonderfully as appetizers.

1 Cut the ends off the plantains and make a slit down the side with the tip of a sharp knife, then peel off the hard skin with your hand. Cut the plantains into 4cm/1½ in chunks.

2 Pour the oil into a deep pan and place it over medium-high heat. When the oil is hot (about 160°C/325°F), add the plantain chunks and deep-fry for 6–8 minutes, turning once if necessary so that they are evenly browned. When cooked, remove the plantains from the oil with a slotted spoon.

3 Spread a sheet of clear film (plastic wrap) on the work surface, put a plantain chunk on it and cover with another piece of clear film. With a heavy pan, pound on the cooked chunk until it is flat and very thin (3–5mm/⅛–¼ in). Repeat with the remaining chunks.

4 Increase the heat of the oil to 180°C/350°F and fry again for 2 minutes on each side. Remove them with a slotted spoon, drain on kitchen paper and sprinkle salt over them immediately. Serve straight away.

Makes 8–10

2 green plantains

750ml/1¼ pints/3 cups oil
  for deep-frying

5ml/1 tsp salt

Cook's tip You can also make lacy fritters called arañitas (literally 'little spiders') by coarsely grating green plantain and dropping it by the spoonful into the hot oil – try it!

Energy 107kcal/450kJ; Protein 1g; Carbohydrate 19g, of which sugars 5g; Fat 4g, of which saturates 0g; Cholesterol 0mg; Calcium 2mg; Fibre 0.9g; Sodium 198mg

Plantain pie
Torta de plátano

This is one of my favourite side dishes. It is very sweet and full of flavour. Here it is baked as one large pie, but you can also use muffin tins to make individual portions. Although a sweet cake, torta de plátano is traditionally eaten with meat, but is also often served at parties, cut into squares. Some cooks add arequipe, the Colombian version of dulce de leche, which makes it irresistible.

1 Preheat the oven to 180°C/350°F/Gas 4. Butter a 20 x 30cm/8 x 12in baking tin (pan) and dust with flour.

2 Cut the ends off the plantains, peel them and cut the flesh into 5mm/¼in dice.

3 Heat the oil in a deep, heavy pan to about 180°C/350°F and deep-fry the plantains for 2–3 minutes, until dark brown but not burned.

4 When cooked, remove the plantains from the pan, with a slotted spoon, drain on kitchen paper and set aside.

5 Put the milk, eggs, flour, butter, sugar, salt and vanilla extract in a food processor, and blend to a smooth batter.

6 Add the fried plantains to the processor, together with the grated cheese and guava paste. Pulse briefly so that it combines but retains a mushy consistency. Transfer the mixture to the prepared baking tin.

7 Bake the pie in the oven for approximately 25–30 minutes, until firm when pressed. Cut into squares and serve warm or cooled.

Cook's tip The plantains for this dish have to be very ripe: almost black, but still firm to the touch. If they feel mushy inside, the taste will be rancid and overripe. Green plantains can take 7–10 days to ripen, so it's better to buy them fully or nearly ripe. They should be stored at room temperature, not chilled.

Serves 12

5 very ripe plantains

475ml/16fl oz/2 cups oil for deep frying

475ml/16fl oz/2 cups milk

2 eggs

75g/3oz/⅔ cup plain (all-purpose) flour, plus extra for dusting

50g/2oz/4 tbsp butter, plus extra for greasing

10ml/2 tsp sugar

10ml/2 tsp salt

2.5ml/½ tsp vanilla extract

225g/8 oz/1¼ cups grated queso blanco (farmer's cheese) or feta

350g/12oz guava paste, cut into dice

Energy 276kcal/115kJ; Protein 5g; Carbohydrate 27g, of which sugars 7g; Fat 17g, of which saturates 6g; Cholesterol 61mg; Calcium 86mg; Fibre 2.2g; Sodium 642mg

Stewed cassava
Yuca guisada

This creamy cooked cassava is bathed in butter and soft cheese, which melts over the hot vegetable to create a simple sauce. This side dish is lovely served with chargrilled meats and salad, or with roast beef or chicken.

1 Place the cassava pieces in a pan with 1.5 litres/2½ pints/6¼ cups water and salt.

2 Bring to the boil, cover and cook for about 50 minutes, or until fork tender. Test with the point of a knife; it should be tender all the way through and will look very mushy at the edges.

3 Drain the cassava, then melt the butter in the hot pan. Return the cassava pieces to the pan and roll to coat in the melted butter. Transfer the cassava to a serving dish.

4 Sprinkle the buttered cassava with the grated cheese, and serve at once as the cheese melts.

Serves 6

1.2kg/2½lb cassava, peeled and quartered

10ml/2 tsp salt

50g/2 oz/¼ cup butter, softened

225g/8 oz queso blanco (white farmer's cheese), grated (see Cook's tip)

Cook's tip If you can't get hold of the Colombian-style cheese, queso blanco, you can use a good quality mozzarella instead.

Energy 455kcal/1920kJ; Protein 8g; Carbohydrate 74g, of which sugars 3g; Fat 16g, of which saturates 11g; Cholesterol 43mg; Calcium 174mg; Fibre 3.2g; Sodium 874mg

Rice with Cheese
Arroz con queso

Serves 4–6

30ml/2 tbsp oil

2 spring onions (scallions), thinly sliced

2–3 green ají dulce chillies, finely chopped

2.5ml/½ tsp salt

400g/14oz/2 cups white long grain rice

1 litre/1¾ pints/4 cups hot water

225g/8oz queso blanco (farmer's cheese), feta or Parmesan cheese, grated

This rice is prepared with a very dry and hard form of white fresh cheese. It can also be made with feta or Parmesan. It is a delicious mixture of cheese, peppers and rice, and can be eaten as a side dish or served with eggs to make a whole meal.

1 Heat the oil over medium heat, add the spring onions, chillies and salt, and sauté for 1 minute.

2 Add the rice to the pan and sauté for 1 minute more, then pour on the hot water, stir and bring to the boil.

3 Simmer until you can see the rice at the surface of the water.

4 Reduce the heat to a minimum, cover and cook for 10 minutes, until the liquid is absorbed and the rice is almost tender.

5 Add the cheese to the pan, and stir in with a fork. Cover the pan again and cook for another 5 minutes. When the cheese is melted, remove the pan from the heat, fluff the rice up with a fork, and serve.

Energy 396kcal/1668kJ; Protein 11g; Carbohydrate 58g, of which sugars 1g; Fat 15g, of which saturates 6g; Cholesterol 26mg; Calcium 172mg; Fibre 0.3g; Sodium 707mg

Desserts and Drinks

Colombians and Venezuelans have a very sweet tooth and love to eat their local fruits in the form of desserts and juices every day.

Sweet dishes to feed the soul

The sheer number and variety of fruits growing in Colombia and Venezuela is vast, and runs through the whole colour spectrum. The juices prepared with these delicious ingredients make a mouthwatering treat that pleases both the eye and the palate. Freshly squeezed fruit juice is served with all three main meals of the day and between meals too, during the hot afternoons. The light sweetness and unforgettable aromas of fresh fruit fill the house, spreading out from the kitchen where they are squeezed, simmered to make a delicious concoction, or left to ripen slowly on a large platter.

There are other ways to eat the many fresh fruits of the region. Desserts in Colombia and Venezuela are mostly made from fruit, which is cooked, either with raw sugar (known as panela) or with white sugar. Milk and coconuts are also staple ingredients in most dessert recipes. There is a whole variety of tempting dishes in this chapter, from simple bolitas de tamarind (tamarind balls) to the more elaborate torta de coca navideña (coconut cake), and natilla (raw sugar pudding) both traditionally eaten at Christmas. Soursop, a creamy fresh fruit, is used in various desserts as it goes beautifully with sweet mixtures and is very refreshing. Figs, guavas and passion fruits are also popular simmered in a sugar syrup.

Hot drinks tend to be based on coffee, or fruit teas of all kinds, or maybe the robust local chocolate, blended with aromatic coconut milk. A more unusual protein-rich drink is known as aveda, and is made with oatmeal simmered in milk with spices. This is usually served cold for breakfast.

Middle right: The town of Jaji, Venezuela, in the Andes.
Page 107: Dusk in Puerto Narino on the Amazon, Colombia.

Poached guavas
Cascos de guayaba

Serves 4–6

450g/1lb guavas
450g/1lb/2¼ cups sugar
5ml/1 tsp lime juice

Cook's tip Guavas can be green or pink. The green ones are easier to peel. Touching guavas can tell you when they are ripe as they are softer to the touch and the skin is thinner, so much so that you can almost tell they are pink inside.

This recipe originated in my grandmother's home department of Tolima. It is a delicious way to fill your house with a sweet aroma. Fresh guavas have a unique fragrance, which is enhanced when they are gently and slowly cooked. There is even a book by Gabriel García Márquez called *The Fragrance of Guava*.

1 Peel the guavas, cut them in half lengthways and scrape out the seeds with a spoon.

2 Place the guavas in a heavy pan and cover with 1 litre/1¾ pints/4 cups water. Bring to the boil, then reduce the heat and simmer, covered, for 20 minutes.

3 Add the sugar to the pan and continue to simmer, covered, for 45 minutes.

4 Add the lime juice to the guavas, and cook for another 3 minutes, until the guavas are cooked through and the liquid has reduced to a syrup. If the guavas are ripe, the sauce will be pink.

Energy 315kcal/1345kJ; Protein 1g; Carbohydrate 83g, of which sugars 82g; Fat 0g; Cholesterol 0mg; Calcium 17mg; Fibre 2.8g; Sodium 8mg

Tamarind balls
Bolitas de tamarindo

Sweets like these are usually eaten only on the streets. They are made and sold by women of African descent, who carry large platters on their heads as they walk through the streets and along the beaches offering their wares. They have been kind enough to teach me how to make some of their marvellous concoctions.

1 Make sure you buy tamarind pulp that is a solid paste, with almost no water, and definitely no sugar added. Break the pulp apart into smaller sections with your hands and drop it into the bowl of an electric mixer.

2 Place the paddle attachment on the mixer and, with the motor on minimum speed, slowly add 250g/9oz/1¼ cups of sugar.

3 Spread the remaining sugar on a large, flat plate. Using your hands, form the mixture into 2.5cm/1in balls.

4 Roll the balls in the plate of sugar, until coated. This will stop them sticking together. If you want to store them, cover them in plenty of sugar to keep them separate from each other, otherwise they will stick together.

Makes 12

225g/8 oz tamarind pulp

300g/11oz/1½ cups caster (superfine) sugar

Cook's tip Tamarind pulp contains seeds, which end up in the tamarind balls, so you need to be careful not to swallow them, spit them out as you eat.

Energy 150kcal/638kJ; Protein 1g; Carbohydrate 38g, of which sugars 38g; Fat 0g; Cholesterol 0mg; Calcium 23mg; Fibre 0g; Sodium 1mg

Coconut mounds
Cocadas blancas

Here's another sweet that is sold in the streets and along the beaches by African-Colombian women. One of these culinary artists invited me into her home to learn how to make this and all their other palangana or platter sweets. When these appear during festivals, both Colombians and tourists go crazy for them.

1 Break the coconuts open and remove the white flesh from the shell. Grate the flesh using the largest holes on the grater. (You need in total of about 350ml/12fl oz/1½ cups grated coconut.) Line a baking tray with baking parchment or a silicon sheet.

2 Place a pan over medium-high heat and add the grated coconut, sugar and milk. Cook, stirring constantly, for 10 minutes or until the liquid is absorbed by the coconut strands, and the mixture leaves the bottom of the pan.

3 Using tongs, pick up 2.5cm/1in clumps of the coconut, and set them down, well spaced, on the prepared baking tray.

4 Leave the coconut clumps to set for about 5 minutes, then transfer them to the lined baking sheet on a rack and leave to cool for about 10 minutes.

5 Peel the clumps off the sheet and serve, or store in an airtight container for 3–4 days. They are delicious with iced coffee.

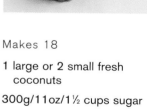

Makes 18

1 large or 2 small fresh coconuts

300g/11oz/1½ cups sugar

120ml/4fl oz/½ cup milk

Cook's tip You can use desiccated (dry shredded) coconut instead of fresh, but if it is the sweetened kind, you will need to reduce the amount of sugar in the recipe by half.

Energy 117kcal/494kJ; Protein 1g; Carbohydrate 18g, of which sugars 18g; Fat 5g, of which saturates 4g; Cholesterol 0mg; Calcium 11mg; Fibre 1g; Sodium 6mg

Orange pastries
Hojaldras

Makes about 48

- 250g/9oz/2¼ cups plain (all-purpose) flour, plus extra for dusting
- 150ml/¼ pint/⅔ cup orange juice
- 30ml/2 tbsp butter
- 15ml/1 tbsp caster (superfine) sugar
- 2.5ml/½ tsp salt
- 1.5ml/¼ tsp baking powder
- 450ml/¾ pint/scant 2 cups oil, for frying
- 50g/2oz/½ cup icing (confectioner's) sugar, for dusting

Hojaldras are popular in many Latin American countries. In Colombia and Venezuela they are made very thin and sprinkled with sugar – in the coastal region this is usually granulated sugar, while cooks in the Andes prefer a dusting of icing sugar.

1 Place the flour, orange juice, butter, caster sugar, salt and baking powder in a food processor and process until it leaves the sides of the bowl and forms a smooth ball of dough. Wrap in plastic and set aside to rest in the refrigerator for 30–45 minutes.

2 On a lightly floured surface, roll out the dough to a thickness of 5mm/¼in (you can use a pasta machine). Cut into strips about 2.5cm/1in wide, then cut diagonally across the strips to form diamond shapes.

3 Heat the oil in a deep pan to 180°C/350°F. Pick up a diamond, lay it on the work surface and roll it again to 2mm/¹⁄₁₆in. It will stick to the rolling pin. Peel it off and fry for 30 seconds per side while you roll the next diamond.

4 As the hojaldras are done, lift them out of the oil and drain on kitchen paper. Dust them with icing sugar and serve immediately.

Cook's tip Hojaldras can be stored for up to a week in an airtight container.

Energy 72kcal/298kJ; Protein 0g; Carbohydrate 5g, of which sugars 2g; Fat 6g, of which saturates 1g; Cholesterol 1mg; Calcium 7mg; Fibre 0.1g; Sodium 23mg

Figs in syrup
Dulce de brevas

Serves 4

450g/1lb fresh figs
2 cinnamon sticks
6 cloves
350g/12oz/1¾ cups sugar
5ml/1 tsp lime juice

Cook's tip Either green or purple figs can be cooked this way. If you use green figs, the end result will be a very pretty transluscent green colour.

Colombians love to eat these figs with some thick arequipe, or dulce de leche, spooned into each quarter, and they can be bought in jars, ready poached and stuffed. An alternative way to serve this delicious dessert is accompanied by cuajada, or fresh white soft cheese, as a contrast to the sweet fruit.

1 Scrape the figs, if necessary, and remove any blemishes with the tip of a knife. Cut into quarters. Place the figs in a heavy pan and cover with 1 litre/1¾ pints/4 cups water.

2 Bring to the boil and cook for 3 minutes, then drain off and discard the water, keeping the figs in the pan. Pour in 1 litre/1¾ pints/4 cups fresh water, and add the cinnamon and cloves. Bring to the boil.

3 Reduce the heat to minimum, cover, and simmer for 30 minutes. Add the sugar to the pan and continue cooking over medium heat, covered, for 1 hour.

4 Stir in the lime juice and cook for 5 minutes more, then remove from the heat.

5 Pour the figs with their syrup into a bowl and leave to cool, then chill until ready to serve.

Energy 361kcal/1540kJ; Protein 0g; Carbohydrate 95g, of which sugars 95g; Fat 0g; Cholesterol 0mg; Calcium 23mg; Fibre 0.6g; Sodium 6mg

Raw sugar pudding
Natilla

Natilla is a very dense, stiff custard, traditionally eaten at Christmas in the mountain region. I remember my first encounter with this sweet, dark-mustard-coloured pudding that did not wobble; it was totally different from what I was used to in the Caribbean. Now it's eaten all over the country, served with a dusting of cinnamon.

1 Heat 1 litre/1¾ pints/4 cups milk in a heavy pan together with the panela or the brown sugar, and the cinnamon stick. Cook over a low heat for 10 minutes. Butter a 20cm/8in square cake tin (pan).

2 Meanwhile, blend 120ml/4fl oz/½ cup milk with the cornflour until the mixture is smooth.

3 Pour the cornflour and milk mixture into the pan and continue to cook, stirring constantly over low heat for 5 minutes, or until the mixture has thickened and you can see the base of the pan when stirring.

4 Add the butter to the thickened mixture and stir until smoothly blended.

5 Remove the cinnamon stick and transfer the mixture to the prepared tin. Leave to cool, then cut into 4cm/1½in squares and dust with ground cinnamon before serving.

Serves 8–12

1 litre/1¾ pints/4 cups whole milk, plus 120ml/4fl oz/½ cup for mixing

225g/8oz panela (raw sugar), grated, or 225g/8oz/1 cup dark brown sugar

1 cinnamon stick, halved

225g/8oz/2 cups cornflour (cornstarch)

25g/1oz/2 tbsp butter, plus extra for greasing

ground cinnamon, to dust

Energy 206kcal/868kJ; Protein 3g; Carbohydrate 39g, of which sugars 21g; Fat 5g, of which saturates 3g; Cholesterol 16mg; Calcium 119mg; Fibre 0g; Sodium 73mg

Soursop mousse

Esponjado de guanábana

The soursop fruit can grow very large – up to 45cm/18in long – and many uses have been found for it in Colombian and Venezuelan cuisine. The juice of the fruit is drunk mixed with water or milk, and the delicious white pulp, which contains numerous black seeds, is turned into desserts such as ice creams, sorbets topped with meringues, and this creamy mousse.

Serves 12

675g/1½lb soursop, seeded and pulped (550ml/18fl oz/2½ cups pulp)

250ml/8fl oz/1 cup whole milk

30ml/2 tbsp powdered gelatine

400g/14oz can sweetened condensed milk

250ml/8fl oz/1 cup double (heavy) cream, chilled

2.5ml/½ tsp vanilla extract

3 egg whites

100g/3½oz/½ cup caster (superfine) sugar

Cook's tip Make sure you pick a ripe soursop, which is a little soft on the outside. Cut the fruit open horizontally; the hard heart of the fruit should be discarded, as should the seeds, only the soft white pulp between the skin and the centre can be eaten.

1 Cut the soursop in half and scoop out the soft pulp with a spoon, transferring it to a bowl. With the tips of your hands feel for the seeds in the pulp. Once you have a seed in your hand, pinch the pulp on one side, and the seed will come out; discard all the seeds this way.

2 Pour the milk into a pan, sprinkle over the gelatine and stir it in. Heat the milk until just warm, stirring until the gelatine is dissolved.

3 Place 400ml/14fl oz/1⅔ cups of soursop pulp in a food processor. Add the milk and gelatine mixture to the processor, together with the condensed milk. Process for 2 minutes. Transfer the mixture to a shallow dish and chill until cold but not set.

4 Pour the cold cream into a mixing bowl with the vanilla extract and whip with a balloon whisk until it holds soft peaks.

5 Take the cold soursop mixture out of the refrigerator, and gently fold it into the whipped cream until mixed thoroughly.

6 Whip the egg whites until stiff. As they start to expand, add the sugar in a slow stream. Keep whisking continuously until the mixture is smooth and glossy.

7 Add a quarter of the egg white mixture to the cool soursop cream and mix well with a spatula.

8 Slowly fold in the remaining egg white, followed by the remaining soursop pulp, until mixed. Transfer the mixture to a serving dish or individual glasses or bowls. Leave to set in the refrigerator until ready to serve.

Energy 292kcal/1221kJ; Protein 5g; Carbohydrate 37g, of which sugars 36g; Fat 15g, of which saturates 9g; Cholesterol 41mg; Calcium 121mg; Fibre 1.9g; Sodium 79mg

Coffee pudding
Flan de café

This kind of baked custard, or flan, is very popular in Colombia and Venezuela. There are several variations, some made with cream cheese or coconut as well as this coffee-flavoured version. Flan de café is always served cold, and makes a great end to any meal.

1 First prepare the coffee, in a small pan bring 350ml/12fl oz/1½ cups water to the boil.

2 Remove from the heat and add the ground coffee, cover and set aside for 3–5 minutes, then strain the coffee mixture through a fine sieve muslin (cheesecloth), and transfer to a large, heavy pan.

3 Add 200g/7oz/1 cup of the sugar to the coffee, stir to mix, bring to the boil and simmer for 7 minutes, or until the mixture has reduced to 250ml/8fl oz/1 cup. Set aside.

4 To prepare the caramel, place the remaining sugar with 250ml/8fl oz/1 cup water in a small, heavy pan. Bring to the boil, stirring until the sugar has dissolved.

5 Lower the heat to medium and cook without stirring for 10–12 minutes, or until it is a light golden colour. Immediately pour the caramel into a 23cm/9in round glass dish or cake tin (pan) and swirl to cover the base. Set aside.

6 Preheat the oven to 150°C/300°F/Gas 2. Beat the eggs in a large bowl, and then mix in the coffee mixture, condensed milk, cream and vanilla extract.

7 Pour the mixture over the caramel in the dish or tin. Set the dish in a roasting pan and pour about 2.5cm/1in water round the dish to make a bain marie. Bake in the oven for 1 hour.

8 Remove the pudding from the oven and leave to cool and set for about 20 minutes. Run a knife around the sides to release it, then place a serving plate over the dish and turn over quickly. Chill until ready to serve.

Serves 12

90g/3½oz/1 cup ground coffee

400g/14oz/2 cups sugar

8 eggs

400g/14oz can sweetened condensed milk

250ml/8fl oz/1 cup double (heavy) cream

5ml/1 tsp vanilla extract

Cook's tip Do not substitute instant coffee for fresh ground coffee, the flavour will not be pleasant. Try to use the best Colombian coffee for a truly authentic flavour.

Energy 406kcal/1705kJ; Protein 8g; Carbohydrate 54g, of which sugars 54g; Fat 19g, of which saturates 10g; Cholesterol 195mg; Calcium 135mg; Fibre 0g; Sodium 110mg

Sugar cookies
Polvorosas

Both adults and children love these little sugar-topped cookies, which are often served during afternoon get-togethers. The little rounds are the most popular shape, but some people make them into half-moons and others cut a little cross into them.

1 Cream the butter with the sugar until very creamy and light. Beat in the vanilla extract.

2 Sift the flour and salt into the bowl, and mix lightly with the butter and sugar mixture to form a soft dough. Chill for 10 minutes, if necessary, to make it easier to handle. Pre-heat the oven to 150°C/300°F/Gas 2. Butter a baking sheet and dust it with a light coating of flour.

3 Form the dough into a log and cut it into 18 pieces. Roll the pieces into balls and make a dent in the centre of each one with your knuckle. Arrange them on the prepared baking sheet and bake for 15–20 minutes.

4 Remove the cookies from the oven and leave to cool on the baking sheet for 5 minutes, then transfer to a rack and dust with icing sugar.

Makes 18

115g/4oz/½ cup butter, plus extra for greasing

100g/3½oz/½ cup sugar

5ml/1 tsp vanilla extract

185g/6½oz/1⅔ cups plain (all-purpose) flour, plus extra for dusting

pinch of salt

25g/1oz/¼ cup icing (confectioner's) sugar

Energy 110kcal/461kJ; Protein 1g; Carbohydrate 15g, of which sugars 7g; Fat 5g, of which saturates 3g; Cholesterol 14mg; Calcium 16mg; Fibre 0.3g; Sodium 61mg

Coconut cake
Torta de coco navideña

Serves 8

flesh from 1 coconut, grated (475ml/16fl oz/2 cups)

200g/7oz/1 cup sugar

120ml/4fl oz/½ cup milk

65g/2½oz/½ cup raisins

225g/8oz sponge cake

50ml/2fl oz/¼ cup sweet wine

3 eggs

2.5ml/½ tsp ground cinnamon

2.5ml/½ tsp vanilla extract

pinch of salt

whipped cream, to serve

This cake is very moist and easy to make, and can be served plain or iced. It is a traditional recipe from the Pacific region, where coconuts are a staple food. The mixture is enriched with sweet wine for celebrations.

1 Place the grated coconut in a pan, add the sugar and milk, and cook, stirring, for 10 minutes until thick and leaving the base of the pan. Stir in the raisins and set aside to cool.

2 Break the cake into pieces in a bowl, sprinkle with the wine and mix with a fork. Set aside.

3 Preheat the oven to 150°C/300°F/Gas 2, butter a 20cm/8in square or round baking tin (pan) and dust it with flour.

4 Beat together the eggs, cinnamon, vanilla and salt until fluffy and light.

5 Stir the coconut mixture into the crumb mixture. Stir in a quarter of the beaten eggs, then fold in the remaining. Add to the prepared tin and bake for 35–40 minutes, or until set.

6 Leave the cake to cool a little, then run a knife around the sides and invert it over a plate. Serve warm or cool, with whipped cream.

Energy 468kcal/1956kJ; Protein 8g; Carbohydrate 50g, of which sugars 45g; Fat 27g, of which saturates 17g; Cholesterol 121mg; Calcium 80mg; Fibre 2.4g; Sodium 130mg

Passion fruit juice
Jugo y sorbete de maracuyá o parchita

Serves 2

3 passion fruit

150ml/¼ pint/⅔ cup water or milk

75ml/5 tbsp sugar

475ml/16fl oz/2 cups ice cubes, crushed

Cook's tip Crush the ice in a food processor, or place the cubes in a plastic bag on a dish towel to prevent it slipping. Then hit repeatedly, with a rolling pin or the base of a heavy pan, until the ice is all crushed.

Passion fruit is a much-loved fruit and the juice makes a tangy, refreshing, semi-sweet drink when crushed ice is added. You can mix it with water, for a long cool drink or with milk for a thicker, frothy and nutritious shake.

1 Cut the passion fruit in half and scoop out the yellow seedy pulp.

2 Place in a blender with the water or milk and blend for 5 seconds.

3 Add the sugar and the crushed ice and blend again until the liquid is smooth.

4 Pass through a sieve and discard the seeds. Transfer to glasses and serve immediately.

Energy 156kcal/664kJ; Protein 1g; Carbohydrate 41g, of which sugars 41g; Fat 0g; Cholesterol 0mg; Calcium 6mg; Fibre 0.7g; Sodium 6mg

Spearmint infusion
Agua aromática de yerbabuena

In Latin America, herbal infusions or teas are often made using fresh leaves picked straight from the garden. There is rarely any need to dry them, as they grow all year round – it's the tropics!

Serves 2

120ml/4fl oz/½ cup fresh
   spearmint leaves
450ml/16fl oz/2 cups water

1 Wash the spearmint leaves well, especially if they are store-bought, as they may have chemical residues on them.

2 Boil the water and pour it into a teapot. Add the mint leaves, reserving a few for decoration, and leave to steep for 2 minutes.

3 Strain the tea into little cups or pretty glasses, and decorate each cup with a couple of reserved mint leaves.

Energy 5kcal/23kJ; Protein 0g; Carbohydrate 1g, of which sugars 0g; Fat 0g; Cholesterol 0mg; Calcium 26mg; Fibre 0g; Sodium 2mg

Fruit and herb infusion
Agua aromática de hierbas y fruta

People normally drink these teas after lunch or dinner, and they are sometimes poured over glasses of colourful fruits.

Serves 4

175ml/6fl oz/¾ cup spearmint
175ml/6fl oz/¾ cup basil
75g/3oz/¾ cup strawberries
75g/3oz/½ cup raspberries
1 green apple, thinly sliced

1 Wash the spearmint and basil leaves. Wash, and hull the strawberries, and cut into halves. Wash the raspberries.

2 Boil 1 litre/1¾ pints/4 cups water in a small pan, and pour it into a pot. Add two-thirds of the spearmint and basil leaves and leave to steep for 2 minutes.

3 Place the prepared fruit in a glass bowl and add the remaining herb leaves.

4 Strain the infusion over the fruit. Cover and take to the table, and let it sit for 2–3 minutes before serving.

Energy 25kcal/105kJ; Protein 1g; Carbohydrate 5g, of which sugars 4g; Fat 0g; Cholesterol 0mg; Calcium 40mg; Fibre 0.8g; Sodium 4mg

Coffee
Tinto, café con leche and pintao

In Latin America, coffee is traditionally brewed in a pot and strained through a cloth filter. First thing in the morning it's usually drunk tinto (black), from a tiny cup, then milk is added for the second, larger, café con leche, at breakfast. Some people prefer just a dash of milk, and will drink pintao, instead of café con leche. Here is how the three types of coffee are made in Colombia.

1 Put the water in a coffee pot and bring to the boil. Turn off the heat and immediately add the ground coffee. Put on the lid and leave to brew for 3–5 minutes.

2 To serve black (café tinto), pour the coffee into small cups through a fine cloth sieve or a regular sieve lined with muslin (cheesecloth).

3 To serve with milk (café con leche), pour equal quantities of coffee and hot milk into a large cup and sweeten to taste.

4 For café pintao (coffee served with a dash of milk) pour 120ml/4fl oz/½ cup coffee into a cup, and add just 10ml/2 tsp hot milk. Sweeten to taste.

Makes 4–6 cups

475ml/16fl oz/2 cups water
120ml/8 tbsp ground coffee
hot milk and sugar to taste
  (optional)

Cook's tip Try to find Colombian coffee beans if you can, and grind them yourself. Colombians are very proud of their coffee, and believe it to be the richest, smoothest coffee in the world. It is grown in the mountains more than 1,500m/5,000ft in altitude and freshened up daily by crystal-clear rivers. The coffee is hand picked only when the bean is red and at its peak of flavour to allow the best-tasting cup possible.

Energy 57kcal/241kJ; Protein 2g; Carbohydrate 6g, of which sugars 0g; Fat 3g, of which saturates 0g; Cholesterol 0mg; Calcium 26mg; Fibre 0g; Sodium 15mg

Hot chocolate
Chocolate caliente

Serves 4

115g/4oz dark (bittersweet) chocolate

1 litre/1¾ pints/4 cups milk, or 500ml/17fl oz/2 cups milk and 500ml/17fl oz/ 2 cups coconut milk

120ml/8 tbsp sugar, or to taste

Colombia produces great chocolate, and Colombians love it, especially in the Andean region, where the climate is colder. Hot chocolate is usually made in a special hourglass-shaped pot, mixed to a froth with a wooden spoon. It is sometimes made with coconut milk.

1 Break up the chocolate and place it with the milk and sugar in a pan over medium heat. Bring to the boil, then reduce the heat to minimum and simmer for 5 minutes, or until all the chocolate has melted.

2 Mix with a wire whisk to froth the milk, and serve immediately.

Energy 350kcal/1481kJ; Protein 6g; Carbohydrate 62g, of which sugars 61g; Fat 11g, of which saturates 6g; Cholesterol 9mg; Calcium 199mg; Fibre 0.7g; Sodium 194mg

Oatmeal drink
Avena

Serves 4–6

75g/3oz/¾ cup fine oatmeal

60–90ml/4–6 tbsp sugar

15ml/1 tbsp cornflour (cornstarch)

2 cinnamon sticks

4 cloves

750ml/1/¼ pints/3 cups milk

ground cinnamon, to serve

This is a delicious drink made with oats and milk, sweetened and spiced with cinnamon and drunk chilled. It's so popular with both children and adults that it's sold ready-made in cartons all over Colombia and Venezuela.

1 Place the oatmeal in a pan with 1 litre/ 1¾ pints/4 cups water, the sugar, cornflour, cinnamon sticks and cloves.

2 Bring to the boil and simmer, stirring continuously, for 3–5 minutes. Remove from the heat and stir in the cold milk. When cool, place in the refrigerator and chill until very cold.

3 To serve, remove the whole spices, pour into glasses, and sprinkle with ground cinnamon.

Energy 172kcal/732kJ; Protein 6g; Carbohydrate 32g, of which sugars 22g; Fat 3g, of which saturates 2g; Cholesterol 7mg; Calcium 158mg; Fibre 0.9g; Sodium 57mg

Useful addresses

UK

La Bodeguita
(Colombian restaurant, deli and online shop)
Elephant & Castle Shopping Centre, London SE1 6TE
Tel : 0207 701 9166
info@labodeguita.co.uk
www.labodeguita.co.uk

Sabor
(Colombian restaurant)
108 Essex Road
London N1 8LX
Tel: 020 7226 5551
www.sabor.co.uk

EUROPE

Bochica Restaurante
(Colombian restaurant)
6 rue Rochebrune 75011
Paris
Tel: (01) 73 71 56 98

Tierra Colombiana
(Colombian restaurant)
Mittenwalder Str. 27
10961 Berlin
Tel: (030) 69 50 79 11
www.tierra-colombiana.com

La Fogata, Casa de Colombia (restaurant)
Glorieta Puente de Segovia1
Madrid
Tel: 91 543 1287
www.lafogatamadrid.com

CANADA

Coco Coqueto
4563 boul. St-Laurent
Montreal, Quebec H2T 1R2
Tel: 514 281 8407

Banano's Cafe
(Colombian and Venezuelan food), 1223 Pacific Blvd.
Vancouver, BC V6Z2R6
Tel: (604) 408-4228

USA

Pueblito, Miami
(Colombian restaurant)
8285 SW 40th Street
Miami, FL 33155
Tel: (305) 551 4650
www.pueblitoviejo.com

Pueblito, Chicago
(Colombian restaurant)
5429 North Lincoln Ave
Chicago, Illinois 60625
Tel: (773) 784 9135

La Pequena Colombia
(Colombian restaurant)
83-87 Roosevelt Avenue
Jackson Heights
New York NY 11372
Tel: (718) 478 8700
www.pequenacolombia.com

Colombian Restaurant
(Restaurants and online shop)
2025 East 7th Ave
Tampa FL 33605
1241 Gulf Boulevard
Clearwater, FL 33767
(727) 596-8400
411 St. Armands Circle
Sarasota, FL 34236
(941) 388-3987
800 2nd Avenue N.E.
St. Petersburg, FL 33701
(727) 822-8000
www.columbiarestaurant.com

Mr Pollo
(Venezuelan restaurant)
2823 Mission St.
San Francisco, CA 94110
Tel: (415) 374 5546
www.mrpollosf.com

Coupa Cafe
(Venezuelan restaurant and coffee shop)
Green Library
571 Escondido Mall
Stanford University, 94305
Tel: (650) 331 0672

Pica Pica Maize Kitchen
(Venezuelan bar and cafe)

Oxbow Public Market
610 First Street, #5
Napa, CA 94559
Tel: (70) 251 3757

El Mercado Latino
(Latin, Colombian and Venezuelan food store)
Seattle,
Washington 98101
Tel: (206) 223 9374
contact@latinmerchant.com

AUSTRALIA

La Cumbia Restaurant
(Colombian restaurant)
14 Gardeners Road
Kingsford 2032, Sydney
(02) 9662 8231

ONLINE

(Colombian food suppliers)
www.amigofoods.com
www.latingourmetproducts.com
www.juanvaldezcoffee.com
(Colombian coffee supplier)
www.latinmerchant.com
(Online latin foods)
www.southamericanwinesonline.co.uk (wine merchants)